VOCA EDGE

S·M·A·R·T

STORYTELLING VOCABULARY

Free MP3 download at www. wearebooks.co.kr

Level 2

We're

Introduction

Every student knows acquiring English vocabulary is a basic necessity for learning the English language. However, not many are aware that simply memorizing vocabulary words is not enough. In order to master a language, students need to spend more time learning how to use these words and what they really mean. Yet, students still spend countless hours memorizing rather than learning.

Even worse is the fact that most vocabulary books are extremely difficult and boring. Fortunately, there is a way for everyone to change their perspective on learning vocabulary. Now you can develop your vocabulary in an enjoyable way. The VOCA EDGE SMART series will help you simultaneously enlarge your vocabulary and improve your English.

This series uses an integrated approach to learning English. Listening, reading, writing and comprehension are all covered in this series.

One of the key features of this series is that it revolves around the daily lives of several characters and the challenges they face in growing up. By reading each episode, students will learn the natural and functional use of English vocabulary.

Each level of this series comes with one textbook and one audio component. Each book is organized into 6 chapters, each of which consists of 2-4 related units. Each book also deals with a variety of unique and interesting topics, and the series is graded to an appropriate length and depth to suit the needs of students with varying levels of English proficiency.

After studying each unit, students will be challenged to review the words and expressions they learned through a series of related questions and activities. Students can listen to the entire script in MP3 format. We invite you to let this series help you take the next step in your journey towards becoming a more proficient speaker of English. We are confident that the VOCA EDGE SMART series can help you make a dramatic improvement in your English ability.

Contents

책의 구성과 특징

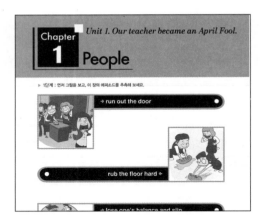

1단계

- Preview 단계로, 주어진 삽화를 보고 각 Unit의 에 피소드를 먼저 추측해볼 수 있습니다.

2단계

- 일기, 대화, 편지 등의 다양한 형태로 제공된 10대 의 일상 생활 속 에피소드를 눈으로 읽고 귀로 듣는 단계로, 어휘뿐만 아니라 Reading 및 Listening, Conversation 학습 효과까지 누릴 수 있습니다.

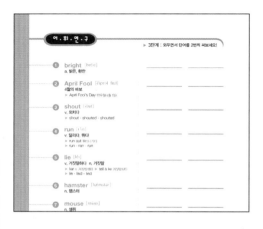

3단계

- 앞의 지문에서 가장 중요한 어휘만을 골라 익히고 연습 하는 단계로, 각 단어와 관련된 유의어 및 반의어, 파 생어를 함께 학습할 수 있습니다.

Exercise

Exercise

A 다음 주어진 단어의 우리말 뜻을 쓰세요.
① bright _____ ② run _____
③ lie _____ ④ bring _____
⑤ break _____ ⑥ anxious _____
⑦ hardly _____ ⑧ balance _____
⑨ ahead _____ ⑩ trick _____

B 다음 우리말 뜻에 해당하는 영어 단어를 쓰세요.
① 4월의 바보 _____
② 외치다 _____
③ 햄스터 _____
④ 붓다 _____

- 중요한 단어 및 표현들을 빈칸에 채워 넣으며, 앞에서 배운 어휘들을 다시 확인하고 점검할 수 있습니다.

Dictation

Date	Score

D 녹음된 내용을 듣고, 다음 빈칸에 들어갈 단어나 표현을 쓰세요.

Dear Diary,

It was a _____, sunny day. ● What a great _____'s Day! ● In English class, we _____ "Look, a mouse!" ● The English teacher ____ out the door. ● But we _____. ● It was just a _____, not a _____. ● One of the kids in class _____ it to school.

During the _____, we _____ oil on the floor. ● We _____ the floor hard. ● We tried to make it _____. ● Finally, the history teacher _____ the classroom. ● I became _____. ● I _____ smiled.

What if he loses his _____ and slips? ● Should I call an _____?

- CD를 듣고 빈칸에 해당하는 단어를 채워 넣으며, Unit의 전체 내용을 복습할 수 있습니다. 또한, 자신의 약점을 파악하여 취약부분만을 집중적으로 학습할 수 있습니다.

Review Test

Review Test (Unit 1~Unit 4)

Total / 30

- 녹음을 듣고, 해당하는 단어와 뜻을 쓰세요.

1	단어:	뜻:	2	단어:	뜻:
3	단어:	뜻:	4	단어:	뜻:
5	단어:	뜻:	6	단어:	뜻:
7	단어:	뜻:	8	단어:	뜻:
9	단어:	뜻:	10	단어:	뜻:

- 각 챕터가 끝나면 앞에서 배운 중요한 단어 30개를 듣고 받아씀으로써, 정확한 발음 공부와 함께 단어 복습도 함께 할 수 있습니다.

Voca Plus

- 영단어들이 어떻게 구성되어 있는지에 대해 어원을 포함한 기본적인 정보들을 배우며, 각 챕터와 관련된 문화 정보와 필수 어휘들도 함께 익힐 수 있습니다.

SMART

Level.2

VOCA EDGE

Chapter 1

People

▶ 1단계 : 먼저 그림을 보고, 이 장의 에피소드를 추측해 보세요.

→ **run out the door**

rub the floor hard ←

→ **lose one's balance and slip**

smile and stop one's tricks ←

Dear Diary,

It was a bright, sunny day. ● What a great April Fool's Day! ● In English class, we shouted "Look, a mouse!" ● The English teacher ran out the door. ● But we lied. ● It was just a hamster, not a mouse. ● One of the kids in class brought it to school.

During the break, we poured oil on the floor. ● We rubbed the floor hard. ● We tried to make it slippery. ● Finally, the history teacher entered the classroom. ● I became anxious. ● I hardly smiled.

What if he loses his balance and slips? ● Should I call an ambulance? ● He neither slipped nor became angry. ● He smiled and stopped our tricks. ● Was he able to think ahead and expect our trick?

1 **bright** [bráit]
a. 밝은, 환한

_____ _____

2 **April Fool** [éiprəl fuːl]
4월의 바보
▶ April Fool's Day 만우절(4월 1일)

_____ _____

3 **shout** [ʃáut]
v. 외치다
▶ shout - shouted - shouted

_____ _____

4 **run** [rʌ́n]
v. 달리다, 뛰다
▶ run out 뛰어나가다
▶ run - ran - run

_____ _____

5 **lie** [lái]
v. 거짓말하다 n. 거짓말
▶ liar n. 거짓말쟁이 ▶ tell a lie 거짓말하다
▶ lie - lied - lied

_____ _____

6 **hamster** [hǽmstər]
n. 햄스터

_____ _____

7 **mouse** [máus]
n. 생쥐

_____ _____

8 **bring** [bríŋ]
v. 가져오다
▶ bring - brought - brought

_____ _____

9 **break** [bréik]
n. 쉬는 시간

_____ _____

10 **pour** [pɔ́ːr]
v. 붓다
▶ pour - poured - poured

_____ _____

11 **rub** [rʌ́b]
v. 문지르다
▶ rub - rubbed - rubbed

_____ _____

▶ 외우면서 단어를 2번씩 써보세요!

⑫ slippery [slípəri]
a. 미끄러운
▶ slip v. 미끄러지다

_____ _____

⑬ enter [éntər]
v. 들어오다
▶ entrance n. 입장, 입구
▶ enter - entered - entered

_____ _____

⑭ anxious [ǽŋkʃəs]
a. 근심하는
▶ anxiety n. 근심

_____ _____

⑮ hardly [háːrdili]
ad. 거의 ~하지 않다
▶ hard ad. 열심히, 세게

_____ _____

⑯ balance [bǽləns]
n. 균형 v. 균형을 잡다
▶ lose one's balance 균형을 잃다
▶ keep one's balance 균형을 유지하다

_____ _____

⑰ ambulance [ǽmbjuləns]
n. 구급차

_____ _____

⑱ slip [slíp]
v. 미끄러지다
▶ slip - slipped - slipped

_____ _____

⑲ stop [stáp]
v. 멈추게 하다 n. 중지
▶ stop - stopped - stopped

_____ _____

⑳ ahead [əhéd]
ad. 앞으로, 앞에

_____ _____

㉑ trick [trík]
n. 장난, 속임수, 재주

_____ _____

Exercise

A 다음 주어진 단어의 우리말 뜻을 쓰세요.

① bright ＿＿＿＿＿＿＿＿ ② run ＿＿＿＿＿＿＿＿
③ lie ＿＿＿＿＿＿＿＿ ④ bring ＿＿＿＿＿＿＿＿
⑤ break ＿＿＿＿＿＿＿＿ ⑥ anxious ＿＿＿＿＿＿＿＿
⑦ hardly ＿＿＿＿＿＿＿＿ ⑧ balance ＿＿＿＿＿＿＿＿
⑨ ahead ＿＿＿＿＿＿＿＿ ⑩ trick ＿＿＿＿＿＿＿＿

B 다음 우리말 뜻에 해당하는 영어 단어를 쓰세요.

① 4월의 바보 ＿＿＿＿＿＿＿＿＿＿＿
② 외치다 ＿＿＿＿＿＿＿＿＿＿＿
③ 햄스터 ＿＿＿＿＿＿＿＿＿＿＿
④ 붓다 ＿＿＿＿＿＿＿＿＿＿＿
⑤ 문지르다 ＿＿＿＿＿＿＿＿＿＿＿
⑥ 미끄러운 ＿＿＿＿＿＿＿＿＿＿＿
⑦ 들어오다 ＿＿＿＿＿＿＿＿＿＿＿
⑧ 구급차 ＿＿＿＿＿＿＿＿＿＿＿
⑨ 미끄러지다 ＿＿＿＿＿＿＿＿＿＿＿
⑩ 생쥐 ＿＿＿＿＿＿＿＿＿＿＿

C 의미가 같도록 알맞은 단어를 넣어 문장을 완성하세요.

1. What a great＿＿＿＿＿＿Day!
   정말 멋진 만우절이었어!

2. The English teacher＿＿＿＿＿＿out the door.
   영어 선생님은 문 밖으로 뛰어나갔어.

3. One of the kids in class＿＿＿＿＿＿it to school.
   반 아이 중 한 명이 학교로 그것을 가져왔어.

4. During the break, we＿＿＿＿＿＿oil on the floor.
   쉬는 시간에 우리는 바닥에 기름을 부었어.

5. We tried to make it＿＿＿＿＿＿.
   우리는 그것을 미끄럽게 하려고 했어.

6. What if he loses his＿＿＿＿＿＿and slips?
   만약 선생님이 균형을 잃고 넘어지시면 어떻게 하지?

7. He neither＿＿＿＿＿＿nor became angry.
   그는 넘어지지도 화를 내지도 않으셨어.

8. Was he able to think＿＿＿＿＿＿and expect our trick?
   그는 앞을 생각하고 우리의 장난을 예상할 수 있었을까?

D 녹음된 내용을 듣고, 다음 빈칸에 들어갈 단어나 표현을 쓰세요. 🎧

Dear Diary,

It was a _____, sunny day. ● What a great _____'s Day! ● In English class, we _____ "Look, a mouse!" ● The English teacher ____ out the door. ● But we _____. ● It was just a _____, not a _____. ● One of the kids in class _____ it to school.

During the _____, we _____ oil on the floor. ● We _____ the floor hard. ● We tried to make it _____. ● Finally, the history teacher _____ the classroom. ● I became _____. ● I _____ smiled.

What if he loses his _____ and slips? ● Should I call an _____? ● He neither _____ nor became angry. ● He smiled and _____ our tricks. ● Was he able to think _____ and expect our _____?

▶ 1단계 : 먼저 그림을 보고, 이 장의 에피소드를 추측해 보세요.

→ **go on a holiday**

exercise before bed ←

→ **quit smoking**

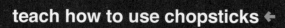
teach how to use chopsticks ←

Bomi: I'm glad mom went on a holiday with her friends.

D a d: Yes, she will be single again for two days!

Bomi: Dad, read this copy. ● It's your New Year's resolutions. ● Mom wants you to sign it.

D a d: "I will exercise before bed." ● "I will stop smoking." ● Ugh, your mom is like my manager!

Bomi: Exercise and you can eat double cheeseburgers sometimes. ● Quit smoking and you can have slices of sweet pies, too. ● By your next checkup, you'll feel much better!

D a d: Your resolution is to help with the chores, right?

Bomi: Yes. Seri, Hoony and I will divide the work. ● I'll take out the garbage. ● Seri will water the plants. ● And Hoony will clean the garage. ● I'm also teaching Hoony how to use chopsticks right now.

D a d: Your mom will be very pleased.

▶ 3단계 : 외우면서 단어를 2번씩 써보세요!

1 **holiday** [hálədèi]
n. 휴일, 휴가
▶ go on a holiday 휴가를 가다

_____ _____

2 **single** [síŋɡəl]
a. 혼자의, 독신의

_____ _____

3 **copy** [kápi]
n. 사본, 복사한 것

_____ _____

4 **resolution** [rèzəlú:ʃən]
n. 결심, 결의
▶ resolute a. 굳게 결심한, 단호한
▶ New Year's resolution 새해 각오(결심)

_____ _____

5 **sign** [sáin]
v. 서명하다
▶ signature n. 서명, 사인
▶ sign - signed - signed

_____ _____

6 **exercise** [éksərsàiz]
v. 운동하다 n. 운동
▶ exercise - exercised - exercised

_____ _____

7 **smoke** [smóuk]
v. 담배를 피우다
▶ smoke - smoked - smoked

_____ _____

8 **like** [làik]
prep. ~와 같이, ~처럼

_____ _____

9 **manager** [mǽnidʒər]
n. 매니저, 관리자

_____ _____

10 **double** [dʌ́bəl]
a. 두 배의, 2중의

_____ _____

▶ 외우면서 단어를 2번씩 써보세요!

⑪ quit [kwít]
v. 그만두다, 끊다
▶ quit - quit - quit

_____   _____

⑫ slice [sláis]
n. 얇게 썬 조각

_____   _____

⑬ checkup [tʃékʌ̀p]
n. 건강 진단

_____   _____

⑭ chores [tʃɔ́ːrz]
n. 가사, 자질구레한 일

_____   _____

⑮ divide [diváid]
v. 나누다
▶ division n. 분배, 분할
▶ divide - divided - divided

_____   _____

⑯ garbage [gáːrbidʒ]
n. 쓰레기

_____   _____

⑰ plant [plǽnt]
n. 식물

_____   _____

⑱ garage [gərɑ́ːʒ]
n. 차고

_____   _____

⑲ chopsticks [tʃápstìks]
n. 젓가락

_____   _____

⑳ pleased [plíːzd]
a. 좋아하는, 기쁜
▶ please v. 기쁘게 하다
▶ pleasure n. 즐거움, 기쁨

_____   _____

Exercise

A 다음 주어진 단어의 우리말 뜻을 쓰세요.

① single _____
② copy _____
③ exercise _____
④ like _____
⑤ manager _____
⑥ double _____
⑦ quit _____
⑧ chores _____
⑨ divide _____
⑩ pleased _____

B 다음 우리말 뜻에 해당하는 영어 단어를 쓰세요.

① 휴일, 휴가 _____
② 결심, 결의 _____
③ 서명하다 _____
④ 담배를 피우다 _____
⑤ 얇게 썬 조각 _____
⑥ 건강 진단 _____
⑦ 쓰레기 _____
⑧ 식물 _____
⑨ 차고 _____
⑩ 젓가락 _____

C 의미가 같도록 알맞은 단어를 넣어 문장을 완성하세요.

1. I'm glad mom went on a_____with her friends.
   저는 엄마가 친구들과 휴가를 떠나서 기뻐요.

2. Mom wants you to_____it.
   엄마는 아빠가 거기에 서명하기를 바라요.

3. Ugh, your mom is_____my manager!
   으, 네 엄마는 내 매니저 같구나!

4. Exercise and you can eat_____cheeseburgers sometimes.
   운동을 하면 가끔 더블 치즈버거를 먹을 수 있어요.

5. _____smoking and you can have slices of sweet pies, too.
   담배를 끊으면 달콤한 파이도 먹을 수 있어요.

6. Your resolution is to help with the_____, right?
   너의 새해 각오는 가사를 돕는 거지, 그렇지?

7. And Hoony will clean the_____.
   그리고 후니는 차고를 청소할 거예요.

8. I'm also teaching Hoony how to use_____right now.
   지금 저는 후니에게 젓가락 사용법을 알려주고도 있어요.

D 녹음된 내용을 듣고, 다음 빈칸에 들어갈 단어나 표현을 쓰세요. 🎧

Bomi: I'm glad mom went on a _____ with her friends.

Dad: Yes, she will be _____ again for two days!

Bomi: Dad, read this _____. • It's your New Year's _____. • Mom
wants you to _____ it.

Dad: "I will _____ before bed." • "I will stop _____." • Ugh, your
mom is _____ my _____!

Bomi: Exercise and you can eat _____ cheeseburgers sometimes. •
_____ smoking and you can have _____ of sweet pies, too. • By
your next _____, you'll feel much better!

Dad: Your resolution is to help with the _____, right?

Bomi: Yes. Seri, Hoony and I will _____ the work. • I'll take out the
_____. • Seri will water the _____. • And Hoony will clean
the _____. • I'm also teaching Hoony how to use _____
right now.

Dad: Your mom will be very _____.

▶ 1단계 : 먼저 그림을 보고, 이 장의 에피소드를 추측해 보세요.

→ have a photo taken

interview someone ←

→ wrap a T-shirt

look from a distance ←

Bomi: Sujin, is this a photo of the Volcanoes, my favorite music band? ● Wow, they are very stylish. ● And Youngwoong is really awesome.

Sujin: I had my photo taken with them. ● My aunt works for a broadcasting company. ● She is a reporter.

Bomi: Does she sometimes interview them?

Sujin: Of course.

Bomi: I really envy her. ● Can she deliver a present for me?

Sujin: Well...

Bomi: I wrapped a T-shirt for Youngwoong. ● And this is a congratulation card for his birthday.

Sujin: Why don't you give it to him in person?

Bomi: You know I'm not brave. ● I don't have the courage to give it to Youngwoong. ● Honestly, I couldn't say anything when I met them before. ● I just looked at them from a distance. ● I don't want to look foolish again.

Sujin boasted a bit in front of me. ● Actually, she knows exactly how much I like the Volcanoes. ● I hope she can help me.

1 **favorite** [féivərit]
a. 좋아하는

_____ _____

2 **stylish** [stáiliʃ]
a. 맵시 있는, 멋진
▶ style n. 스타일

_____ _____

3 **awesome** [ɔ́ːsəm]
a. 멋진, 굉장한
▶ awe n. 경외, 경외심

_____ _____

4 **photo** [fóutou]
n. 사진
▶ photographer n. 사진사

_____ _____

5 **broadcasting** [brɔ́ːdkæstiŋ]
n. 방송

_____ _____

6 **reporter** [ripɔ́ːrtər]
n. 기자
▶ report v. 보도하다 n. 보도, 보고(서)

_____ _____

7 **interview** [íntərvjùː]
v. 인터뷰하다
▶ interview - interviewed -
  interviewed

_____ _____

8 **envy** [énvi]
v. 부러워하다, 질투하다 n. 질투, 선망
▶ envious a. 질투가 많은
▶ envy - envied - envied

_____ _____

9 **deliver** [dilívər]
v. 전하다, 배달하다
▶ delivery n. 배달
▶ deliver - delivered - delivered

_____ _____

10 **wrap** [ræp]
v. 포장하다
▶ wrap - wrapped - wrapped

_____ _____

▶ 외우면서 단어를 2번씩 써보세요!

⑪ congratulation
[kəngrǽtʃəléiʃən]
n. 축하
▶ congratulate v. 축하하다

_____ _____

⑫ person [pə́:rsən]
n. 사람, 개인
▶ personal a. 개인적인 ▶ in person 직접

_____ _____

⑬ brave [bréiv]
a. 용감한
▶ bravery n. 용기 ▶ bravely ad. 용감하게

_____ _____

⑭ courage [kə́:ridʒ]
n. 용기
▶ encourage v. 격려하다
▶ courageous a. 용감한

_____ _____

⑮ honestly [ánistli]
ad. 솔직히
▶ honesty n. 솔직함 ▶ honest a. 솔직한

_____ _____

⑯ distance [dístəns]
n. 먼 거리, 먼 곳, 거리
▶ distant a. 거리가 떨어진, 먼

_____ _____

⑰ foolish [fú:liʃ]
a. 어리석은
▶ fool n. 바보

_____ _____

⑱ boast [bóust]
v. 자랑하다
▶ boastful a. 자랑하는
▶ boast - boasted - boasted

_____ _____

⑲ exactly [igzǽktli]
ad. 정확하게
▶ exact a. 정확한

_____ _____

⑳ help [hélp]
v. 돕다, 거들다   n. 도움
▶ help - helped - helped

_____ _____

Exercise

A 다음 주어진 단어의 우리말 뜻을 쓰세요.

① stylish _____   ② awesome _____
③ reporter _____   ④ envy _____
⑤ deliver _____   ⑥ wrap _____
⑦ person _____   ⑧ distance _____
⑨ boast _____   ⑩ help _____

B 다음 우리말 뜻에 해당하는 영어 단어를 쓰세요.

① 좋아하는 _____
② 사진 _____
③ 방송 _____
④ 인터뷰하다 _____
⑤ 축하 _____
⑥ 용감한 _____
⑦ 용기 _____
⑧ 솔직히 _____
⑨ 어리석은 _____
⑩ 정확하게 _____

C 의미가 같도록 알맞은 단어를 넣어 문장을 완성하세요.

1. I had my_____taken with them.
   나는 그들과 함께 사진을 찍었어.

2. My aunt works for a_____company.
   우리 고모가 방송국에서 일하시거든.

3. Does she sometimes_____them?
   그녀는 가끔 그들을 인터뷰도 해?

4. Can she_____a present for me?
   나 대신 선물을 전해 줄 수 있을까?

5. Why don't you give it to him in_____?
   네가 그에게 직접 주지 그래?

6. I don't have the_____to give it to Youngwoong.
   나는 영웅에게 그것을 줄 용기가 없어.

7. I just looked at them from a_____.
   단지 먼 거리에서 바라만 보았어.

8. Sujin_____a bit in front of me.
   수진은 내 앞에서 약간 자랑했다

D 녹음된 내용을 듣고, 다음 빈칸에 들어갈 단어나 표현을 쓰세요. 🎧

Bomi: Sujin, is this a photo of the Volcanoes, my _____ music band? ●
Wow, they are very _____. ● And Youngwoong is really _____.

Sujin: I had my _____ taken with them. ● My aunt works for a _____
company. ● She is a _____.

Bomi: Does she sometimes _____ them?

Sujin: Of course.

Bomi: I really _____ her. ● Can she _____ a present for me?

Sujin: Well...

Bomi: I _____ a T-shirt for Youngwoong. ● And this is a _____
card for his birthday.

Sujin: Why don't you give it to him in _____?

Bomi: You know I'm not _____. ● I don't have the _____ to give
it to Youngwoong. ● _____, I couldn't say anything when I met
them before. ● I just looked at them from a _____. ● I don't want
to look _____ again.

Sujin _____ a bit in front of me. ● Actually, she knows _____
how much I like the Volcanoes. ● I hope she can _____ me.

▶ 1단계 : 먼저 그림을 보고, 이 장의 에피소드를 추측해 보세요.

→ **move to the same elementary school** ○

○ **sit next to someone** ←

→ **look alike** ○

○ **be good at spreading jam evenly** ←

Dear Sara,

Do you remember when we first met? • We moved to the same elementary school. • We even came to school on the same date. • Naturally we became friends. • Suppose we were not in the same classroom, who would have been my friend? • You sat next to me. • We don't look alike at all, but our classmates said we did. • We are different in some ways. • You have good sense for cooking, but I don't. • I like your toast and you can make it without burning it. • You are also good at spreading jam evenly. • You're a bit shy, but I'm outgoing. You are very friendly to me. • We are similar in some ways, too. • We like the same programs. • During our spare time, we enjoy acting. • Sometimes we pretend we are in a spaceship. • Sara, never forget your promise to go to the South Pole with me in the future.

▶ **3단계 : 외우면서 단어를 2번씩 써보세요!**

1 **remember** [rimémbər]
v. 기억하다
▶ remembrance n. 기억, 추억
▶ remember - remembered - remembered

_____ _____

2 **elementary** [èləméntəri]
a. 초등학교의, 입문의

_____ _____

3 **date** [deit]
n. 날짜
▶ dated a. 날짜가 있는

_____ _____

4 **naturally** [nǽtʃərəli]
ad. 자연스럽게, 당연히
▶ nature n. 자연 ▶ natural a. 자연스러운

_____ _____

5 **suppose** [səpóuz]
v. 가정하다, 만약 ~이면, 어떨까
▶ suppose - supposed - supposed

_____ _____

6 **alike** [əláik]
a. 비슷한, 서로 같은

_____ _____

7 **classmate** [klǽsmèit]
n. 반친구, 급우

_____ _____

8 **different** [dífərənt]
a. 다른
▶ difference n. 차이(점)
▶ differently ad. 다르게

_____ _____

9 **sense** [séns]
n. 감각
▶ sensory a. 감각의
▶ sensitive a. 민감한
▶ sensible a. 분별 있는, 느낄 수 있는

_____ _____

10 **burn** [bə́ːrn]
v. 태우다
▶ burn - burned/burnt - burned/ burnt

_____ _____

▶ 외우면서 단어를 2번씩 써보세요!

11 spread [sprèd]
v. 바르다, 펴다
▶ spread - spread - spread

_____   _____

12 evenly [íːvənli]
ad. 고르게, 평평하게
▶ even a. 평평한, 고른

_____   _____

13 outgoing [áutgòuiŋ]
a. 외향적인

_____   _____

14 friendly [fréndli]
a. 친절한
▶ friend n. 친구

_____   _____

15 similar [símələr]
a. 유사한
▶ similarity n. 유사함

_____   _____

16 program [próugræm]
n. 프로그램

_____   _____

17 during [djúəriŋ]
prep. ~동안

_____   _____

18 spare [spɛər]
a. 여분의

_____   _____

19 sometimes [sʌ́mtàimz]
ad. 가끔

_____   _____

20 spaceship [spéisʃip]
n. 우주선

_____   _____

21 forget [fərgét]
v. 잊다
▶ forgetful a. 잘 잊어버리는
▶ forgettable a. 잊기 쉬운

_____   _____

22 future [fjúːtʃər]
n. 미래, 앞날

_____   _____

Exercise

A 다음 주어진 단어의 우리말 뜻을 쓰세요.

① elementary _____ ② naturally _____
③ suppose _____ ④ spread _____
⑤ evenly _____ ⑥ outgoing _____
⑦ during _____ ⑧ sometimes _____
⑨ alike _____ ⑩ future _____

B 다음 우리말 뜻에 해당하는 영어 단어를 쓰세요.

① 기억하다 _____
② 반친구, 급우 _____
③ 다른 _____
④ 감각 _____
⑤ 태우다 _____
⑥ 친절한 _____
⑦ 유사한 _____
⑧ 여분의 _____
⑨ 우주선 _____
⑩ 잊다 _____

C 의미가 같도록 알맞은 단어를 넣어 문장을 완성하세요.

1. We even came to school on the same_____.
   심지어 같은 날짜에 학교에 왔어.

2. _____ we were not in the same classroom, who would have been my friend?
   만일 우리가 같은 학급이 아니었으면, 누가 내 친구가 되었을까?

3. We don't look _____ at all, but our classmates said we did.
   우리는 생김새가 닮지 않았는데, 우리 반 애들은 우리가 그렇다고 말했어.

4. You have good _____ for cooking, but I don't.
   너는 요리에 감각이 있지만, 나는 없어.

5. You are also good at _____ jam evenly.
   너는 또한 잼을 고르게 바르는 것을 잘해.

6. You're a bit shy, but I'm _____.
   너는 약간 부끄러움을 타지만, 나는 외향적이야.

7. We are _____ in some ways, too.
   우리는 어떤 점에서는 비슷해.

8. _____ we pretend we are in a spaceship.
   가끔 우리는 우주선을 탄 척을 하지.

D 녹음된 내용을 듣고, 다음 빈칸에 들어갈 단어나 표현을 쓰세요.

Dear Sara,

Do you _____ when we first met? ● We moved to the same _____ school. ● We even came to school on the same _____. ● _____ we became friends. ● _____ we were not in the same classroom, who would have been my friend? ● You sat next to me. ● We don't look _____ at all, but our _____ said we did. ● We are _____ in some ways. ● You have good _____ for cooking, but I don't. ● I like your toast and you can make it without _____ it. ● You are also good at _____ jam _____. ● You're a bit shy, but I'm _____. You are very _____ to me. ● We are _____ in some ways, too. ● We like the same _____. ● _____ our _____ time, we enjoy acting. ● _____ we pretend we are in a _____. ● Sara, never forget your _____ to go to the South Pole with me in the _____.

Test (Unit 1~Unit 4)

■ 녹음을 듣고, 해당하는 단어와 뜻을 쓰세요.

1	단어:	뜻:	2	단어:	뜻:
3	단어:	뜻:	4	단어:	뜻:
5	단어:	뜻:	6	단어:	뜻:
7	단어:	뜻:	8	단어:	뜻:
9	단어:	뜻:	10	단어:	뜻:
11	단어:	뜻:	12	단어:	뜻:
13	단어:	뜻:	14	단어:	뜻:
15	단어:	뜻:	16	단어:	뜻:
17	단어:	뜻:	18	단어:	뜻:
19	단어:	뜻:	20	단어:	뜻:
21	단어:	뜻:	22	단어:	뜻:
23	단어:	뜻:	24	단어:	뜻:
25	단어:	뜻:	26	단어:	뜻:
27	단어:	뜻:	28	단어:	뜻:
29	단어:	뜻:	30	단어:	뜻:

Voca Plus

Appearance

1. **curly hair** 곱슬머리
2. **straight hair** 직모
3. **T-shirt** 티셔츠
4. **skirt** 치마
5. **suit** 정장
6. **high heels** 하이힐
7. **sneakers** 운동화
8. **handbag** 핸드백
9. **shoulder bag** 어깨에 매는 가방
10. **blouse** 블라우스
11. **dress shirt** 정장용 셔츠
12. **tie** 타이

Culture Plus

Personalities 성격

+ **dynamic** 동적인	+ **outgoing** 외향적인
+ **bold** 대담한	+ **selfish** 이기적인
+ **cheerful** 쾌활한	+ **shy** 수줍음을 타는, 내성적인
+ **diligent** 부지런한	+ **talkative** 수다스런
+ **friendly** 친절한, 다정한	+ **timid** 소심한, 겁 많은
+ **gentle** 신사다운	+ **witty** 재치가 있는

SMART

Level.2

VOCA EDGE

Chapter 2

History, Art, and Culture

▶ 1단계 : 먼저 그림을 보고, 이 장의 에피소드를 추측해 보세요.

→ cut one's finger

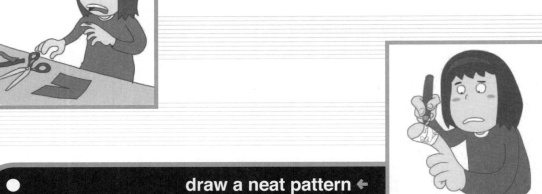

draw a neat pattern ←

→ add some beads

send a picture ←

▶ 2단계 : 녹음 내용을 들으며, 추측한 에피소드와 비교해 보세요.

S e r i : Ouch, I cut my finger. ● Look, there is blood!

Bomi : I'll get the first-aid kit. ● Here, put this bandage on it.

S e r i : That one is so plain and simple. ● I'm going to draw something on it.

Bomi : Why don't you draw some hot dogs?

S e r i : That's gross. ● No, I'll draw a really neat pattern. ● Isn't it beautiful?
　　　　● And I want to add some beads.

Bomi : I'll help you glue them on.

S e r i : Thanks. Hey, get the digital camera for me.

Bomi : Are you going to post a picture on YouTube?

S e r i : No, I want to send it to a bandage company. ● It might impress them.

Bomi : I guess it could help their business.

▶ 3단계 : 외우면서 단어를 2번씩 써보세요!

1 cut [kʌ́t]
v. 베다, 상처를 내다
n. 베기
▶ cut - cut - cut

_____   _____

2 blood [blʌ́d]
n. 피
▶ bleed v. 피가 나다

_____   _____

3 first-aid [fə́:rst-eid]
a. 응급 치료의

_____   _____

4 bandage [bǽndidʒ]
n. 반창고

_____   _____

5 plain [pléin]
a. 평범한, 단조로운

_____   _____

6 simple [símpəl]
a. 단순한, 간단한
▶ simplify v. 간단하게 하다

_____   _____

7 draw [drɔ́:]
v. 그리다
▶ draw - drew - drawn

_____   _____

8 hot dog [hɑ́t dɔ̀(:)g]
n. 핫도그

_____   _____

9 gross [gróus]
a. 불쾌한, 구역질 나는

_____   _____

10 pattern [pǽtərn]
n. 무늬

_____   _____

11 beautiful [bjú:təfəl]
a. 아름다운
▶ beauty n. 아름다움

_____   _____

12 **add** [ǽd]
v. 추가하다, 더하다
▶ add - added - added

_____ _____

13 **glue** [glúː]
v. 접착제로 붙이다
n. 접착제
▶ glue - glued – glued

_____ _____

14 **digital camera**
[dídʒitl kǽmərə]
디카(디지털 카메라)

_____ _____

15 **post** [póust]
v. 게시하다, 정보를 알리다
▶ post - posted - posted

_____ _____

16 **send** [sénd]
v. 보내다
▶ send - sent - sent

_____ _____

17 **company** [kʌ́mpəni]
n. 회사

_____ _____

18 **impress** [imprés]
v. 깊은 인상을 주다
▶ impression n. 인상
▶ impressive a. 인상적인
▶ impress - impressed - impressed

_____ _____

19 **guess** [gés]
v. 추측하다, 알아맞히다
▶ guess - guessed - guessed

_____ _____

20 **business** [bíznis]
n. 사업

_____ _____

Exercise

A 다음 주어진 단어의 우리말 뜻을 쓰세요.

① cut　＿＿＿＿＿＿＿＿　② plain　＿＿＿＿＿＿＿＿

③ simple　＿＿＿＿＿＿＿＿　④ gross　＿＿＿＿＿＿＿＿

⑤ add　＿＿＿＿＿＿＿＿　⑥ glue　＿＿＿＿＿＿＿＿

⑦ post　＿＿＿＿＿＿＿＿　⑧ impress　＿＿＿＿＿＿＿＿

⑨ guess　＿＿＿＿＿＿＿＿　⑩ first-aid　＿＿＿＿＿＿＿＿

B 다음 우리말 뜻에 해당하는 영어 단어를 쓰세요.

① 피　＿＿＿＿＿＿＿＿＿＿＿

② 반창고　＿＿＿＿＿＿＿＿＿＿＿

③ 그리다　＿＿＿＿＿＿＿＿＿＿＿

④ 핫도그　＿＿＿＿＿＿＿＿＿＿＿

⑤ 무늬　＿＿＿＿＿＿＿＿＿＿＿

⑥ 아름다운　＿＿＿＿＿＿＿＿＿＿＿

⑦ 디지털 카메라　＿＿＿＿＿＿＿＿＿＿＿

⑧ 보내다　＿＿＿＿＿＿＿＿＿＿＿

⑨ 회사　＿＿＿＿＿＿＿＿＿＿＿

⑩ 사업　＿＿＿＿＿＿＿＿＿＿＿

C 의미가 같도록 알맞은 단어를 넣어 문장을 완성하세요.

1. I'll get the ＿＿＿＿＿ kit.
   내가 구급상자를 가져올게.

2. Here, put this ＿＿＿＿＿ on it.
   자 여기, 거기에 이 반창고를 붙여.

3. That one is so ＿＿＿＿＿ and ＿＿＿＿＿.
   그것은 너무 평범하고 단순해.

4. No, I'll draw a really neat ＿＿＿＿＿.
   아니, 나는 아주 멋진 무늬를 그릴 거야.

5. I'll help you ＿＿＿＿＿ them on.
   네가 그걸 붙일 수 있게 도와줄게.

6. Thanks. Hey, get the ＿＿＿＿＿ for me.
   고마워. 내게 디카를 가져다 줘.

7. Are you going to ＿＿＿＿＿ a picture on YouTube?
   유튜브에 사진을 올릴 거니?

8. I ＿＿＿＿＿it could help their business.
   나는 그것이 그들의 사업에 도움이 될 수 있을 거라고 생각해.

D 녹음된 내용을 듣고, 다음 빈칸에 들어갈 단어나 표현을 쓰세요. 🎧

Seri: Ouch, I _____ my finger. ● Look, there is _____!

Bomi: I'll get the _____ kit. ● Here, put this _____ on it.

Seri: That one is so _____ and _____ . ● I'm going to _____ something on it.

Bomi: Why don't you draw some hot _____?

Seri: That's _____. ● No, I'll draw a really neat _____. ● Isn't it _____? ● And I want to _____ some beads.

Bomi: I'll help you _____ them on.

Seri: Thanks. Hey, get the _____ for me.

Bomi: Are you going to _____ a picture on YouTube?

Seri: No, I want to _____ it to a bandage _____. ● It might _____ them.

Bomi: I _____ it could help their _____.

▶ 1단계 : 먼저 그림을 보고, 이 장의 에피소드를 추측해 보세요.

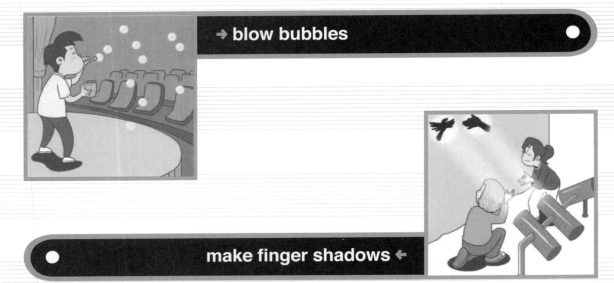

→ **blow bubbles**

make finger shadows ←

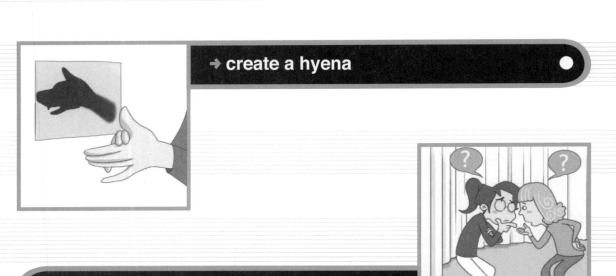

→ **create a hyena**

use one's brain ←

Dear Diary,

I see Hoony blowing soap bubbles. ● I'll count them. ● He blew ten round bubbles. ● He also blew some flat bubbles. ● He can make other shapes, too. ● He is practicing for his bubble show. ● Sara and I are going to make finger shadows for him. ● We will also be his voice actors. ● We are going to be behind a screen.

Bomi : The show is going to be on schedule, right? ● Watch us create a hyena.

Hoony: Are those its sharp teeth?

Bomi : Yes, it's eating rotten meat. ● The meat bone was hard to make.

Hoony: Yeah, you really used your brains!

Bomi : Now, look at us make tree branches.

Hoony: Neat! Oh, look at all the students at the gate.

Bomi : Don't worry. They'll think you're a professional!

▶ 3단계 : 외우면서 단어를 2번씩 써보세요!

1 blow [blóu]
v. 불다
▶ blow - blew - blown

_____ _____

2 bubble [bʌ́bəl]
n. 거품

_____ _____

3 count [káunt]
v. 세다, 계산하다
▶ countable a. 셀 수 있는
▶ count - counted - counted

_____ _____

4 round [ráund]
a. 둥근

_____ _____

5 flat [flǽt]
a. 납작한

_____ _____

6 shape [ʃéip]
n. 모양

_____ _____

7 practice [prǽktis]
v. 연습하다 n. 연습
▶ practice - practiced - practiced

_____ _____

8 shadow [ʃǽdou]
n. 그림자

_____ _____

9 voice actor [vóis ǽktər]
성우

_____ _____

10 screen [skríːn]
n. 막, 휘장

_____ _____

11 schedule [skédʒu(ː)l]
n. 예정, 계획
▶ on schedule 예정대로
▶ ahead schedule 예정보다 먼저
▶ behind schedule 예정보다 늦게

_____ _____

▶ 외우면서 단어를 2번씩 써보세요!

12 create [kriéit]

v. 만들어내다, 창작하다
- ▶ creation n. 창작, 작품
- ▶ creative a. 창조적인, 독창적인
- ▶ create - created - created

_____ _____

13 sharp [ʃáːrp]

a. 날카로운

_____ _____

14 rotten [rátn]

a. 썩은
- ▶ rot v. 썩다, 부패하다

_____ _____

15 bone [bóun]

n. 뼈

_____ _____

16 brain [bréin]

n. 뇌
- ▶ use one's brain 머리를 쓰다, 지혜를 짜내다

_____ _____

17 branch [brǽntʃ]

n. 가지

_____ _____

18 student [stʃúːdənt]

n. 학생

_____ _____

19 gate [géit]

n. 출입문

_____ _____

20 professional [prəféʃənəl]

n. 전문가 a. 프로의

_____ _____

Exercise

A 다음 주어진 단어의 우리말 뜻을 쓰세요.

① count ＿＿＿＿＿＿　② shape ＿＿＿＿＿＿
③ practice ＿＿＿＿＿＿　④ screen ＿＿＿＿＿＿
⑤ schedule ＿＿＿＿＿＿　⑥ create ＿＿＿＿＿＿
⑦ sharp ＿＿＿＿＿＿　⑧ branch ＿＿＿＿＿＿
⑨ rotten ＿＿＿＿＿＿　⑩ professional ＿＿＿＿＿＿

B 다음 우리말 뜻에 해당하는 영어 단어를 쓰세요.

① 불다 ＿＿＿＿＿＿＿＿＿＿
② 거품 ＿＿＿＿＿＿＿＿＿＿
③ 둥근 ＿＿＿＿＿＿＿＿＿＿
④ 납작한 ＿＿＿＿＿＿＿＿＿＿
⑤ 그림자 ＿＿＿＿＿＿＿＿＿＿
⑥ 성우 ＿＿＿＿＿＿＿＿＿＿
⑦ 뼈 ＿＿＿＿＿＿＿＿＿＿
⑧ 뇌 ＿＿＿＿＿＿＿＿＿＿
⑨ 학생 ＿＿＿＿＿＿＿＿＿＿
⑩ 출입문 ＿＿＿＿＿＿＿＿＿＿

C 의미가 같도록 알맞은 단어를 넣어 문장을 완성하세요.

1. I see Hoony ＿＿＿＿＿ soap bubbles.
   후니가 비눗방울을 부는 모습이 보여.

2. He is ＿＿＿＿＿ for his bubble show.
   그는 자신의 비눗방울 쇼를 위해 연습하고 있어.

3. Sara and I are going to make finger ＿＿＿＿＿ for him.
   사라와 나는 그를 위해 손가락 그림자를 만들어 줄 거야.

4. We will also be his ＿＿＿＿＿.
   우리는 그의 성우도 되어 줄 거야.

5. The show is going to be on ＿＿＿＿＿, right?
   쇼는 예정대로 진행될 거지, 그렇지?

6. The meat ＿＿＿＿＿ was hard to make.
   고기 뼈는 표현하기 힘들었어.

7. Yeah, you really used your ＿＿＿＿＿!
   그래, 정말 머리를 썼네!

8. Don't worry. They'll think you're a ＿＿＿＿＿!
   걱정하지 마. 그들은 네가 전문가라고 생각할 거야!

D 녹음된 내용을 듣고, 다음 빈칸에 들어갈 단어나 표현을 쓰세요. 🎧

Dear Diary,

I see Hoony _____ soap _____. ● I'll _____ them. ● He blew ten _____ bubbles. ● He also blew some _____ bubbles. ● He can make other _____, too. ● He is _____ for his bubble show. ● Sara and I are going to make finger _____ for him. ● We will also be his _____. ● We are going to be behind a _____.

Bomi: The show is going to be on _____, right? ● Watch us _____ a hyena.

Hoony: Are those its _____ teeth?

Bomi: Yes, it's eating _____ meat. ● The meat _____ was hard to make.

Hoony: Yeah, you really used your _____!

Bomi: Now, look at us make tree _____.

Hoony: Neat! Oh, look at all the _____ at the _____.

Bomi: Don't worry. They'll think you're a _____!

▶ 1단계 : 먼저 그림을 보고, 이 장의 에피소드를 추측해 보세요.

→ **life in the past**

make one's first flight ←

→ **invent the telephone**

change conversations ←

Dear Diary,

Grandpa and I talked about life in the past. ● I asked him about some changes that occurred in the last century. ● He explained some of them to me.

Grandpa: We didn't go to the dentist to pull out teeth. ● Can you imagine pulling them out at home?

B o m i : Oh, the pain! ● Wasn't it harmful to people's health?

Grandpa: Not at all. ● And we didn't get regular checkups, either. ● There were many historical events in the 20th century. ● The Wright brothers made their first flight.

B o m i : So they were the world's first pilots.

Grandpa: Yes. Cars began to be mass-produced. ● Workers made them in factories. ● Before, there were lots of farmers. ● But soon, there were more factory engineers.

B o m i : And the telephone was a big change in communication, right?

Grandpa: Well, Alexander Graham Bell invented that a century earlier. ● In the 20th century, cell phones changed conversations.

▶ 3단계 : 외우면서 단어를 2번씩 써보세요!

1 **past** [pæst]
n. 과거

_____ _____

2 **occur** [əkə́:r]
v. 일어나다, 발생하다
▶ occurrence n. 발생, 사건
▶ occur - occurred - occurred

_____ _____

3 **century** [séntʃuri]
n. 세기, 100년

_____ _____

4 **explain** [ikspléin]
v. 설명하다
▶ explanation n. 설명
▶ explanatory a. 설명적인
▶ explain - explained - explained

_____ _____

5 **dentist** [déntist]
n. 치과 의사

_____ _____

6 **imagine** [imǽdʒin]
v. 상상하다
▶ imagination n. 상상
▶ imaginary a. 상상의, 가상의
▶ imaginative a. 상상력이 풍부한
▶ imagine - imagined - imagined

_____ _____

7 **pain** [péin]
n. 고통
▶ painful a. 고통스러운

_____ _____

8 **harmful** [hɑ́:rmfəl]
a. 해로운
▶ harm v. 해를 주다 n. 해로움

_____ _____

9 **regular** [régjələr]
a. 정기적인

_____ _____

10 **historical** [histɔ́(:)rikəl]
a. 역사적인
▶ history n. 역사

_____ _____

▶ 외우면서 단어를 2번씩 써보세요!

11 flight [fláit]
n. 비행
▶ fly v. 날다

_____ _____

12 pilot [páilət]
n. 조종사

_____ _____

13 mass-produce
[mǽs prədjúːs]
v. 대량 생산하다
▶ mass-produced a. 대량 생산의
▶ mass-produce - mass-produced
  - mass-produced

_____ _____

14 factory [fǽktəri]
n. 공장

_____ _____

15 farmer [fáːrmər]
n. 농부

_____ _____

16 engineer [èndʒəniər]
n. 기술자

_____ _____

17 communication
[kəmjùːnəkéiʃən]
n. 의사 소통
▶ communicate v. 의사 소통하다

_____ _____

18 invent [invént]
v. 발명하다
▶ invention n. 발명
▶ inventor n. 발명가
▶ invent - invented -invented

_____ _____

19 earlier [ə́ːrliər]
ad. 일찍이, 예전에

_____ _____

20 conversation
[kànvərséiʃən]
n. 대화
▶ converse v. 이야기하다

_____ _____

Exercise

A 다음 주어진 단어의 우리말 뜻을 쓰세요.

① occur ＿＿＿＿＿＿＿
③ imagine ＿＿＿＿＿＿＿
⑤ harmful ＿＿＿＿＿＿＿
⑦ invent ＿＿＿＿＿＿＿
⑨ farmer ＿＿＿＿＿＿＿

② century ＿＿＿＿＿＿＿
④ mass-produce ＿＿＿＿＿＿＿
⑥ explain ＿＿＿＿＿＿＿
⑧ earlier ＿＿＿＿＿＿＿
⑩ engineer ＿＿＿＿＿＿＿

B 다음 우리말 뜻에 해당하는 영어 단어를 쓰세요.

① 과거 ＿＿＿＿＿＿＿＿＿
② 치과 의사 ＿＿＿＿＿＿＿＿＿
③ 고통 ＿＿＿＿＿＿＿＿＿
④ 역사적인 ＿＿＿＿＿＿＿＿＿
⑤ 비행 ＿＿＿＿＿＿＿＿＿
⑥ 조종사 ＿＿＿＿＿＿＿＿＿
⑦ 공장 ＿＿＿＿＿＿＿＿＿
⑧ 의사 소통 ＿＿＿＿＿＿＿＿＿
⑨ 대화 ＿＿＿＿＿＿＿＿＿
⑩ 정기적인 ＿＿＿＿＿＿＿＿＿

C 의미가 같도록 알맞은 단어를 넣어 문장을 완성하세요.

1. I asked him about some changes that ＿＿＿＿＿＿ in the last century.
   나는 그에게 지난 세기에 있었던 변화에 대해 여쭤봤어.

2. He ＿＿＿＿＿＿ some of them to me.
   그는 내게 몇 가지에 대해 설명해 주었어.

3. Can you ＿＿＿＿＿＿ pulling them out at home?
   집에서 그것을 뽑았다는 게 상상이 되니?

4. There were many ＿＿＿＿＿＿ events in the 20th century.
   20세기에는 역사적인 사건이 많았어.

5. Yes. Cars began to be ＿＿＿＿＿＿.
   맞아. 자동차가 대량생산되기 시작했어.

6. And the telephone was a big change in ＿＿＿＿＿＿, right?
   그리고 전화기가 의사 소통에 있어서 큰 변화였어요, 그렇죠?

7. Well, Alexander Graham Bell invented that a century ＿＿＿＿＿＿.
   음, 알렉산더 그레이엄 벨은 한 세기 앞서 그것을 발명했어.

8. In the 20th century, cell phones changed ＿＿＿＿＿＿.
   20세기에는, 휴대 전화가 대화를 바꿔놓았어.

D 녹음된 내용을 듣고, 다음 빈칸에 들어갈 단어나 표현을 쓰세요. 🎧

Dear Diary,

Grandpa and I talked about life in the _____. ● I asked him about some changes that _____ in the last _____. ● He _____ some of them to me.

···

Grandpa: We didn't go to the _____ to pull out teeth. ● Can you _____ pulling them out at home?

B o m i : Oh, the _____! ● Wasn't it _____ to people's health?

Grandpa: Not at all. ● And we didn't get _____ checkups, either. ● There were many _____ events in the 20th century. ● The Wright brothers made their first _____.

B o m i : So they were the world's first _____.

Grandpa: Yes. Cars began to be _____. ● Workers made them in _____. ● Before, there were lots of _____. ● But soon, there were more factory _____.

B o m i : And the telephone was a big change in _____, right?

Grandpa: Well, Alexander Graham Bell _____ that a century _____. ● In the 20th century, cell phones changed _____.

■ **녹음을 듣고, 해당하는 단어와 뜻을 쓰세요.**

1	단어:	뜻:	2	단어:	뜻:
3	단어:	뜻:	4	단어:	뜻:
5	단어:	뜻:	6	단어:	뜻:
7	단어:	뜻:	8	단어:	뜻:
9	단어:	뜻:	10	단어:	뜻:
11	단어:	뜻:	12	단어:	뜻:
13	단어:	뜻:	14	단어:	뜻:
15	단어:	뜻:	16	단어:	뜻:
17	단어:	뜻:	18	단어:	뜻:
19	단어:	뜻:	20	단어:	뜻:
21	단어:	뜻:	22	단어:	뜻:
23	단어:	뜻:	24	단어:	뜻:
25	단어:	뜻:	26	단어:	뜻:
27	단어:	뜻:	28	단어:	뜻:
29	단어:	뜻:	30	단어:	뜻:

Voca Plus

On Halloween

1. **pumpkin** 늙은 호박
2. **jack-o-lantern** 호박 초롱
3. **candle** 양초
4. **witch** 마녀
5. **broom** 빗자루
6. **trick or treat** 사탕 안주면 장난칠 거야
7. **mask** 가면
8. **candy** 사탕
9. **pirate** 해적
10. **costume party** 여러 가지 복장의 파티
11. **treats** 선물로 주는 사탕
12. **ghost** 유령

Special Days 특별한 날

+ **Christmas** 크리스마스   + **Columbus Day** 콜럼버스의 날

+ **Parents' Day** 어버이의 날   + **Arbor Day** 식목일

+ **April Fool's Day** 만우절   + **Memorial Day** 현충일

+ **New Year's Day** 새해 첫날

+ **Thanksgiving Day** 추수 감사절

+ **Independence Day** 독립기념일

VOCA EDGE

Chapter 3 Politics and Social Issues

▶ 1단계 : 먼저 그림을 보고, 이 장의 에피소드를 추측해 보세요.

→ **take a shower with hot water**

an oil spill ←

→ **rinse off rocks**

show one's appreciation ←

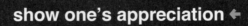

D a d: Tomorrow we will leave for an ocean village. ● It's far from Seoul.

Bomi: Dad, can we take a shower with hot water? ● Can we have delicious seafood there?

D a d: Bomi, we're going to volunteer there.

Bomi: Pardon? ● Volunteering on Christmas Eve? ● Dad, are you talking like Jesus, "Love your neighbors?"

D a d: Bomi, there was an oil spill.

Dad announced the news suddenly at dinner. ● We reached the village in the early morning. ● Many people were rinsing off rocks. ● Our family worked like a team.

I found some birds on the coast. ● Seri and I did pair work. ● We cleaned oil from their feathers. ● We worked hard and even skipped a meal. ● At the end of the day, the villagers showed their appreciation to us. ● Dad said, "Bomi and Seri, you were really hardworking today. I'm proud of you."

▶ 3단계 : 외우면서 단어를 2번씩 써보세요!

① **village** [vílidʒ]
n. 마을
▶ villager 마을 사람

_____   _____

② **far** [fáːr]
a. 먼

_____   _____

③ **shower** [ʃáuər]
n. 샤워
v. 샤워하다, 잔뜩 주다
▶ take a shower 샤워하다

_____   _____

④ **seafood** [síːfúːd]
n. 해산물

_____   _____

⑤ **volunteer** [váləntíər]
v. 자원 봉사하다
n. 자원자
▶ volunteer - volunteered -
volunteered

_____   _____

⑥ **pardon** [páːrdn]
v. 용서하다 n. 용서
▶ pardon - pardoned - pardoned

_____   _____

⑦ **eve** [íːv]
n. 전날 밤

_____   _____

⑧ **neighbor** [néibər]
n. 이웃(사람)
▶ neighborhood n. 이웃, 동네
▶ neighboring a. 이웃의, 근접한

_____   _____

⑨ **oil spill** [ɔ́il spil]
기름 유출

_____   _____

⑩ **announce** [ənáuns]
v. 알리다, 발표하다
▶ announcement n. 발표, 공고
▶ announce - announced - announced

_____   _____

▶ 외우면서 단어를 2번씩 써보세요!

11 **dinner** [dínər]
n. 식사, 정찬
_____ _____

12 **reach** [ríːtʃ]
v. ~에 도착하다
▶ reachable a. 닿을 수 있는
▶ reach - reached - reached
_____ _____

13 **rinse** [ríns]
v. 씻어내다, 헹구다
▶ rinse - rinsed - rinsed
_____ _____

14 **team** [tíːm]
n. 단체, 팀 v. 팀을 이루다
_____ _____

15 **coast** [kóust]
n. 해안
▶ coastal a. 해안의
_____ _____

16 **pair** [péər]
n. 한 쌍, 2인조
_____ _____

17 **feather** [féðər]
n. 깃털
_____ _____

18 **meal** [míːl]
n. 식사
_____ _____

19 **appreciation** [əpriːʃiéiʃən]
n. 감사
▶ appreciate v. 감사하다
_____ _____

20 **really** [ríːəli]
ad. 정말로, 실제로
_____ _____

21 **hardworking** [háːrdwə̀ːrkiŋ]
a. 열심히 일하는
_____ _____

Exercise

A 다음 주어진 단어의 우리말 뜻을 쓰세요.

① shower _____
② volunteer _____
③ pardon _____
④ announce _____
⑤ rinse _____
⑥ reach _____
⑦ pair _____
⑧ hardworking _____
⑨ far _____
⑩ oil spill _____

B 다음 우리말 뜻에 해당하는 영어 단어를 쓰세요.

① 마을 _____
② 전날 밤 _____
③ 이웃(사람) _____
④ 식사, 정찬 _____
⑤ 해안 _____
⑥ 깃털 _____
⑦ 감사 _____
⑧ 식사 _____
⑨ 해산물 _____
⑩ 팀을 이루다, 단체 _____

C 의미가 같도록 알맞은 단어를 넣어 문장을 완성하세요.

1. Tomorrow we will leave for an ocean _____.
   내일 우리는 해안 마을로 떠날 거야.

2. Volunteering on Christmas _____?
   크리스마스 전날 밤에 자원 봉사를 한다고요?

3. Dad, are you talking like Jesus, "Love your _____?"
   아빠, 지금 예수님처럼 "네 이웃을 사랑하라"고 말씀하시는 거예요?

4. Dad _____ the news suddenly at dinner.
   아빠는 갑자기 저녁 식사 때 그것을 알리셨다.

5. Many people were _____ off rocks.
   많은 사람들이 돌들을 씻어내고 있었다.

6. I found some birds on the _____.
   나는 해안에서 몇 마리의 새들을 발견했다.

7. We worked hard and even skipped a _____.
   우리는 열심히 일했고 식사조차 걸렀다.

8. At the end of the day, the villagers showed their _____ to us.
   하루가 끝날 무렵에, 마을 사람들은 우리에게 감사를 표시했다.

D 녹음된 내용을 듣고, 다음 빈칸에 들어갈 단어나 표현을 쓰세요. ○

Dad: Tomorrow we will leave for an ocean _____. ● It's _____ from Seoul.

Bomi: Dad, can we take a _____ with hot water? ● Can we have delicious _____ there?

Dad: Bomi, we're going to _____ there.

Bomi: _____? ● Volunteering on Christmas _____ ? ● Dad, are you talking like Jesus, "Love your _____?"

Dad: Bomi, there was an oil _____.

Dad _____ the news suddenly at _____. ● We _____ the village in the early morning. ● Many people were _____ off rocks. ● Our family worked like a _____.

I found some birds on the _____. ● Seri and I did _____ work. ● We cleaned oil from their _____. ● We worked hard and even skipped a _____. ● At the end of the day, the villagers showed their _____ to us. ● Dad said, "Bomi and Seri, you were _____ _____ today. I'm proud of you."

▶ 1단계 : 먼저 그림을 보고, 이 장의 에피소드를 추측해 보세요.

→ **make hair too firm**

be not allowed to wear loose pants ←

→ **look at the handout**

like hair dyed purple ←

S e r i: Let's use my hair spray.

Bomi: Hey, you're making my hair too firm.

S e r i: Bomi, why do you always wear either a black or a gray coat? ● Why do you wear a skirt on cold days?

Bomi: We can't wear loose pants at school.

S e r i: That's unfair. ● Someday I will design school uniforms for girls.

Bomi: Seri, look at this handout. ● It's about our school regulations.

S e r i: You underlined some parts. ● What's this rule for? ● Colorful coats are not allowed? ● Now I understand the reason. ● That's why you wear such boring coats. ● Even Sara's pet likes her hair dyed purple.

Bomi: Right. I want to express my personality. ● Why aren't middle school students allowed to do so?

① **spray** [spréi]
n. 스프레이
v. 뿌리다

② **firm** [fə́ːrm]
a. 단단한, 굳은
n. 회사
▶ firmly ad. 단단하게

③ **either** [íːðər]
conj. ~거나 ~거나
a. 둘 중 하나의
▶ either A or B A 또는 B

④ **skirt** [skə́ːrt]
n. 치마

⑤ **loose** [lúːs]
a. 헐렁한
▶ loosen v. 헐렁하게 하다

⑥ **unfair** [ʌnfɛ́ər]
a. 불공평한
▶ fair a. 공평한

⑦ **uniform** [júːnəfɔ̀ːrm]
n. 제복, 교복

⑧ **handout** [hǽndàut]
n. 유인물

⑨ **regulation** [règjəléiʃən]
n. 규정
▶ regulate v. 규제하다

⑩ **underline** [ʌ́ndərlain]
v. 밑줄을 긋다 n. 밑줄
▶ underline - underlined - underlined

⑪ **rule** [ru:l]
n. 규칙 v. 지배하다

_____ _____

⑫ **colorful** [kʌ́lərfəl]
a. 다채로운, 화려한
▶ color n. 색

_____ _____

⑬ **reason** [rí:zən]
n. 이유 v. 설명하다
▶ reasonable a. 합당한

_____ _____

⑭ **boring** [bɔ́:riŋ]
a. 지루한

_____ _____

⑮ **dye** [dai]
v. 염색하다
▶ dyed a. 염색된
▶ dye - dyed - dyed

_____ _____

⑯ **purple** [pə́:rpəl]
a. 자주빛의, 보라빛의

_____ _____

⑰ **express** [iksprés]
v. 표현하다
▶ expression n. 표현
▶ expressive a. 표현적인
▶ express - expressed - expressed

_____ _____

⑱ **personality** [pə̀:rsənǽləti]
n. 개성
▶ express one's personality
   개성을 표현하다

_____ _____

⑲ **middle** [mídl]
a. 가운데의
▶ middle school 중학교

_____ _____

⑳ **allow** [əláu]
v. 허가하다, 허락하다
▶ allowance n. 허용, 허락
▶ allow - allowed - allowed

_____ _____

Exercise

A 다음 주어진 단어의 우리말 뜻을 쓰세요.

① spray _____   ② firm _____
③ either _____   ④ uniform _____
⑤ underline _____   ⑥ rule _____
⑦ colorful _____   ⑧ reason _____
⑨ purple _____   ⑩ allow _____

B 다음 우리말 뜻에 해당하는 영어 단어를 쓰세요.

① 치마 _____
② 헐렁한 _____
③ 불공평한 _____
④ 유인물 _____
⑤ 규정 _____
⑥ 지루한 _____
⑦ 염색하다 _____
⑧ 표현하다 _____
⑨ 개성 _____
⑩ 가운데의 _____

C 의미가 같도록 알맞은 단어를 넣어 문장을 완성하세요.

1. Hey, you're making my hair too _____.
   이봐, 너는 내 머리를 너무 단단하게 만들고 있어.

2. We can't wear _____ pants at school.
   우리는 학교에 헐렁한 바지를 입고 갈 수 없어.

3. Someday I will design school _____ for girls.
   언젠가 나는 여자아이들을 위한 교복을 디자인할 거야.

4. It's about our school _____.
   우리 학교의 규칙들이야.

5. What's this _____ for?
   이 규칙은 왜 있는 거야?

6. Even Sara's pet likes her hair _____ purple.
   심지어 사라의 애완 동물도 털을 보라색으로 염색하는 걸 좋아해.

7. Right. I want to _____ my _____.
   맞아. 나는 나의 개성을 표현하고 싶어.

8. Why aren't middle school students _____ to do so?
   왜 중학생들은 그렇게 하는 것이 허용이 안 되지?

D 녹음된 내용을 듣고, 다음 빈칸에 들어갈 단어나 표현을 쓰세요. 🎧

Seri: Let's use my hair _____.

Bomi: Hey, you're making my hair too _____.

Seri: Bomi, why do you always wear _____ a black or a gray coat? ●
Why do you wear a _____ on cold days?

Bomi: We can't wear _____ pants at school.

Seri: That's _____. ● Someday I will design school _____ for girls.

Bomi: Seri, look at this _____. ● It's about our school _____.

Seri: You _____ some parts. ● What's this _____ for? ● _____
coats are not allowed? ● Now I understand the _____. ● That's
why you wear such _____ coats. ● Even Sara's pet likes her hair
_____.

Bomi: Right. I want to _____ my _____. ● Why aren't _____
school students _____ to do so?

▶ 1단계 : 먼저 그림을 보고, 이 장의 에피소드를 추측해 보세요.

→ **have a message**

have peace ←

→ **use more gestures**

no borders between countries ←

▶ 2단계 : 녹음 내용을 들으며, 추측한 에피소드와 비교해 보세요.

Sara: Bomi, I like this song, Imagine. ● It has a message. ● Why not add some lines to it?

Bomi: I agree. ● Imagine if there was no war. ● We wouldn't need any soldiers.

Sara: But who would protect our country?

Bomi: Just imagine if there were no weapons.

Sara: Then, we would have peace. ● There wouldn't be any borders between countries.

Bomi: Imagine if there was no language.

Sara: We would use more gestures. ● Imagine if there was no map.

Bomi: Then, we wouldn't have enough knowledge about the world.

Sara: We wouldn't be able to locate where the deserts are.

Bomi: Imagine if there was no education. ● We would have difficulty understanding everything.

1 imagine [imædʒin]
v. 상상하다
▶ imagination n. 상상력
▶ imaginary a. 상상의
▶ imagine - imagined - imagined

2 message [mésidʒ]
n. 메시지

3 line [láin]
n. 가사

4 agree [əgríː]
v. 동의하다
▶ agreement n. 동의
▶ agreeable a. 기분 좋은, 동의하는
▶ agree - agreed - agreed

5 war [wɔ́ːr]
n. 전쟁

6 soldier [sóuldʒər]
n. 군인

7 protect [prətékt]
v. 보호하다, 지키다
▶ protection n. 보호
▶ protective a. 보호하는
▶ protect - protected - protected

8 weapon [wépən]
n. 무기
▶ weaponize v. 무기화하다

9 peace [piːs]
n. 평화
▶ peaceful a. 평온한

10 border [bɔ́ːrdər]
n. 국경

▶ 외우면서 단어를 2번씩 써보세요!

⑪ between [bitwíːn]
prep. ~사이에

_____   _____

⑫ language [læŋgwidʒ]
n. 언어

_____   _____

⑬ gesture [dʒéstʃər]
n. 몸짓

_____   _____

⑭ map [mǽp]
n. 지도

_____   _____

⑮ enough [ináf]
a. 충분한

_____   _____

⑯ knowledge [nálidʒ]
n. 지식
  ▶ knowledgeable a. 지식 있는, 식견이 있는

_____   _____

⑰ desert [dézəːrt]
n. 사막
a. 사막 같은, 불모의
v. 버리다

_____   _____

⑱ education [édʒukèiʃən]
n. 교육
  ▶ educational a. 교육적인

_____   _____

⑲ difficulty [dífikλlti]
n. 어려움
  ▶ difficult a. 어려운
  ▶ have difficulty ~ing ~하는 데 어려움을 겪다

_____   _____

Exercise

A 다음 주어진 단어의 우리말 뜻을 쓰세요.

① imagine _____   ② agree _____
③ soldier _____   ④ protect _____
⑤ between _____   ⑥ gesture _____
⑦ enough _____   ⑧ desert _____
⑨ difficulty _____ ⑩ weapon _____

B 다음 우리말 뜻에 해당하는 영어 단어를 쓰세요.

① 메시지 _____
② 가사 _____
③ 평화 _____
④ 국경 _____
⑤ 언어 _____
⑥ 지도 _____
⑦ 지식 _____
⑧ 교육 _____
⑨ 전쟁 _____
⑩ 충분한 _____

C 의미가 같도록 알맞은 단어를 넣어 문장을 완성하세요.

1. Why not add some _____ to it?
   노래에 가사를 더 추가하는 게 어때?

2. Imagine if there was no _____.
   전쟁이 없다고 상상해 봐.

3. There wouldn't be any _____ between countries.
   나라 사이의 국경도 없을 거야.

4. We would use more _____.
   우리는 몸짓을 더 사용하게 될 거야.

5. Then, we wouldn't have _____ knowledge about the world.
   그러면, 우리는 세상에 대한 충분한 지식이 없을 거야.

6. We wouldn't be able to locate where the _____ are.
   사막이 어디에 있는지 알 수 없을 거야.

7. We would have _____ understanding everything.
   우리는 모든 것을 이해하는 데 어려움이 있을 거야.

8. But who would _____ country?
   하지만 누가 우리나라를 지키지?

D 녹음된 내용을 듣고, 다음 빈칸에 들어갈 단어나 표현을 쓰세요.

Sara: Bomi, I like this song, _____. ● It has a _____. ● Why not add some _____ to it?

Bomi: I _____. ● Imagine if there was no _____. ● We wouldn't need any _____.

Sara: But who would protect _____ country?

Bomi: Just imagine if there were no _____.

Sara: Then, we would have _____. ● There wouldn't be any _____ _____ countries.

Bomi: Imagine if there was no _____.

Sara: We would use more _____. ● Imagine if there was no _____.

Bomi: Then, we wouldn't have _____ _____ about the world.

Sara: We wouldn't be able to locate where the _____ are.

Bomi: Imagine if there was no _____. ● We would have _____ understanding everything.

■ 녹음을 듣고, 해당하는 단어와 뜻을 쓰세요.

1	단어:	뜻:	2	단어:	뜻:
3	단어:	뜻:	4	단어:	뜻:
5	단어:	뜻:	6	단어:	뜻:
7	단어:	뜻:	8	단어:	뜻:
9	단어:	뜻:	10	단어:	뜻:
11	단어:	뜻:	12	단어:	뜻:
13	단어:	뜻:	14	단어:	뜻:
15	단어:	뜻:	16	단어:	뜻:
17	단어:	뜻:	18	단어:	뜻:
19	단어:	뜻:	20	단어:	뜻:
21	단어:	뜻:	22	단어:	뜻:
23	단어:	뜻:	24	단어:	뜻:
25	단어:	뜻:	26	단어:	뜻:
27	단어:	뜻:	28	단어:	뜻:
29	단어:	뜻:	30	단어:	뜻:

Voca Plus

At a park

1. **ride a bike** 자전거 타다
2. **make loud noises** 소음을 내다
3. **throw trash** 쓰레기를 버리다
4. **cover one's ears** 귀를 막다
5. **walk one's dog** 개를 산책시키다
6. **pick flowers** 꽃을 꺾다

Culture Plus

Environment 환경

+ **pollution** 오염

+ **water pollution** 수질 오염

+ **air pollution** 공기 오염

+ **oil spill** 기름 유출

+ **disposable** 일회용품

+ **plastic bag** 비닐봉지

+ **recycling** 재활용

+ **recycling bin** 재활용 통

SMART

Level.2

VOCA EDGE

Chapter 4

Economy

Chapter 4
Economy

Unit 11. We discuss how to save money.

▶ 1단계 : 먼저 그림을 보고, 이 장의 에피소드를 추측해 보세요.

→ **talk on the wireless phone** ○

○ **go shopping** ←

→ **use store coupons** ○

○ **unplug things** ←

D a d: Let's discuss how we can save money.

Bomi: I have a good example. ● Seri, don't talk so long on the wireless phone.

S e r i: Ha! Don't chat so long on your cell phone, Bomi!

D a d: And when should we make international calls?

Bomi: Late at night. ● They are cheaper then.

Mom: And I'll try to go shopping in the late afternoon. ● Goods are cheaper then.

S e r i: And go to the outdoor market, right?

Mom: Yes. Goods are cheaper there than at the department stores. ● But make use of department store sales.

Bomi: I always try to use store coupons.

Hoony: I know how to save electricity. ● Turn off lights. ● And unplug things when they're not in use.

Mom: Wow, you are all so wise about saving money!

▶ 3단계 : 외우면서 단어를 2번씩 써보세요!

1 save [séiv]
v. 절약하다, 아끼다
▶ saving n. 절약 a. 절약하는
▶ save - saved - saved

_____   _____

2 money [mʌ́ni]
n. 돈, 화폐

_____   _____

3 example [igzǽmpəl]
n. 보기, 예

_____   _____

4 wireless [wáiərlis]
a. 무선의
▶ wire n. 전선, 전화선

_____   _____

5 chat [tʃǽt]
v. 수다를 떨다
n. 잡담, 담소
▶ chat - chatted - chatted

_____   _____

6 international [ìntərnǽʃənəl]
a. 국제적인, 국제간의
▶ make an international call 국제 전화하다

_____   _____

7 night [nait]
n. 밤

_____   _____

8 cheaper [tʃíːpər]
a. 값이 더 싼
▶ cheap a. 값이 싼
▶ cheapest a. 값이 가장 싼

_____   _____

9 shopping [ʃápiŋ]
n. 쇼핑, 물건 사기, 장보기
▶ go shopping 쇼핑하러 가다, 장보러 가다

_____   _____

10 goods [gúdz]
n. 상품, 물품

_____   _____

▶ 외우면서 단어를 2번씩 써보세요!

11 **outdoor** [áutdɔ̀ːr]
a. 야외의

_____ _____

12 **market** [máːrkit]
n. 시장
▶ outdoor market n. 재래시장

_____ _____

13 **department store**
[dipáːrtmənt stɔ̀ːr]
백화점

_____ _____

14 **sale** [séil]
n. 세일, 할인행사

_____ _____

15 **coupon** [kjúːpɑn / -pɔn]
n. 쿠폰, 할인권

_____ _____

16 **electricity** [ilèktrísəti]
n. 전기

_____ _____

17 **turn** [tə́ːrn]
v. 돌리다
▶ turn off (불. 전등 등을) 끄다
▶ turn on (불. 전등 등을) 켜다
▶ turn - turned - turned

_____ _____

18 **light** [láit]
n. 빛, 등불

_____ _____

19 **unplug** [ʌnplʌ́g]
v. 플러그를 뽑다
▶ plug in v. 플러그를 꽂다
▶ plug n. 플러그
▶ unplug - unplugged - unplugged

_____ _____

20 **wise** [wáiz]
a. 현명한, 박식한
▶ wisdom n. 지혜

_____ _____

Exercise

A 다음 주어진 단어의 우리말 뜻을 쓰세요.

① example _____　② wireless _____
③ international _____　④ chat _____
⑤ shopping _____　⑥ goods _____
⑦ unplug _____　⑧ wise _____
⑨ sale _____　⑩ save _____

B 다음 우리말 뜻에 해당하는 영어 단어를 쓰세요.

① 밤 _____
② 값이 더 싼 _____
③ 야외의 _____
④ 시장 _____
⑤ 백화점 _____
⑥ 전기 _____
⑦ 돌리다 _____
⑧ 빛, 등불 _____
⑨ 돈, 화폐 _____
⑩ 쿠폰, 할인권 _____

C 의미가 같도록 알맞은 단어를 넣어 문장을 완성하세요.

1. Let's discuss how we can _____ money.
   돈을 절약할 수 있는 방법에 대해 의논하자.

2. Seri, don't talk so long on the _____ phone.
   세리, 무선 전화기로 오래 통화하지 마.

3. And when should we make _____ calls?
   그리고 국제 전화는 언제 하는 것이 좋지?

4. And go to the _____ market, right?
   그리고 재래시장에 가야죠, 그렇죠?

5. Yes. Goods are cheaper there than at the _____.
   그래. 그곳 물건이 백화점에서보다 더 싸단다.

6. But make use of department store _____.
   하지만 백화점 세일을 활용해야지.

7. I know how to save _____.
   저는 전기를 아끼는 방법을 알아요.

8. And _____ things when they're not in use.
   그리고 사용하지 않을 때는 플러그를 빼요.

D 녹음된 내용을 듣고, 다음 빈칸에 들어갈 단어나 표현을 쓰세요.

D a d : Let's discuss how we can _____ _____.

Bomi: I have a good _____. ● Seri, don't talk so long on the _____ phone.

D a d : Ha! Don't _____ so long on your cell phone, Bomi!

D a d : And when should we make _____ calls?

Bomi: Late at _____. ● They are _____ then.

Mom : And I'll try to _____ in the late afternoon. ● _____ are cheaper then.

S e r i : And go to the _____ _____, right?

Mom : Yes. Goods are cheaper there than at the _____. ● But make use of department store _____.

Bomi: I always try to use store _____.

Hoony: I know how to save _____. ● _____ off _____. ● And _____ things when they're not in use.

Mom : Wow, you are all so _____ about saving money!

▶ 1단계 : 먼저 그림을 보고, 이 장의 에피소드를 추측해 보세요.

→ **ride a skateboard**

get prize money ←

→ **hate standing on the skateboard**

have something as a reward ←

Bomi: I can't buy a ticket to the Volcanoes' concert. ● I can't spend over 50,000 won on it.

Sara: I can't afford one, either. ● They are so expensive!

Bomi: Hey, look at that ad ● That dog is riding a skateboard.

Sara: It says they are picking new models. ● The winners get prize money. ● We should enter Brownie!

Bomi: Yes, let's get her to pose on this skateboard.

Sara: Put these sunglasses on her. ● Good. I'll take her photograph.

Bomi: Ugh! Brownie hates standing on the skateboard. ● Calm down, Brownie. ● I don't want to anger you. ● I'm begging you, Brownie!

Sara: Yes, I finally got it! ● Excellent, Brownie!

Bomi: Great, we succeeded! ● Good job, Brownie!

Sara: Here, have some tuna as a reward.

Bomi: Have some milk, Brownie. ● You look thirsty.

▶ 3단계 : 외우면서 단어를 2번씩 써보세요!

1 ticket [tíkit]
n. 표, 입장권

_____ _____

2 concert [kánsə(:)rt / kón-]
n. 콘서트, 음악회

_____ _____

3 spend [spénd]
v. 쓰다, 소비하다 n. 지출, 비용
▶ spend - spent - spent

_____ _____

4 afford [əfɔ́ːrd]
v. ～할 여유가 있다
▶ affordable a. 줄 수 있는, (가격이) 알맞은
▶ afford - afforded - afforded

_____ _____

5 expensive [ikspénsiv]
a. 비싼

_____ _____

6 ad [ǽd]
n. 광고 (advertisement의 줄임말)

_____ _____

7 skateboard [skéitbɔ̀ːrd]
n. 스케이트보드

_____ _____

8 model [mάdl]
n. 모델

_____ _____

9 prize [praiz]
n. 상, 포상
▶ prize money 상금

_____ _____

10 enter [éntər]
v. (경기 등에) 참가시키다
▶ enter - entered - entered

_____ _____

11 pose [póuz]
v. 자세(포즈)를 취하다
n. 자세(포즈)
▶ pose - posed - posed

_____ _____

▶ 외우면서 단어를 2번씩 써보세요!

12 sunglasses [sʌ́ŋglæ̀siz]
n. 선글라스

_____ _____

13 photograph [fóutəgræ̀f]
n. 사진 v. 사진을 찍다
▶ take a photograph 사진을 찍다

_____ _____

14 hate [héit]
v. 몹시 싫어하다
▶ hatred n. 증오, 미움
▶ hate - hated - hated

_____ _____

15 stand [stǽnd]
v. 서다, 일어서다
▶ stand - stood – stood

_____ _____

16 anger [ǽŋgər]
v. 화나게 하다 n. 노여움, 화
▶ anger - angered - angered

_____ _____

17 beg [bég]
v. 빌다, 간청하다
▶ beg - begged - begged

_____ _____

18 excellent [éksələnt]
a. 훌륭한
▶ excellence n. 우수, 훌륭함

_____ _____

19 succeed [səksíːd]
v. 성공하다
▶ success n. 성공
▶ succeed - succeeded - succeeded

_____ _____

20 job [dʒáb]
n. 임무 완수, 역할

_____ _____

21 reward [riwɔ́ːrd]
n. 보수, 보상
▶ rewardless a. 무보수의, 헛수고의

_____ _____

22 thirsty [θə́ːrsti]
a. 목마른, 갈망하는
▶ thirst n. 갈증

_____ _____

Exercise

A 다음 주어진 단어의 우리말 뜻을 쓰세요.

① ticket _____   ② spend _____
③ afford _____   ④ enter _____
⑤ pose _____   ⑥ photograph _____
⑦ anger _____   ⑧ beg _____
⑨ job _____   ⑩ thirsty _____

B 다음 우리말 뜻에 해당하는 영어 단어를 쓰세요.

① 비싼 _____
② 스케이트보드 _____
③ 상, 포상 _____
④ 몹시 싫어하다 _____
⑤ 서다, 일어서다 _____
⑥ 훌륭한 _____
⑦ 성공하다 _____
⑧ 보수, 보상 _____
⑨ 콘서트, 음악회 _____
⑩ 광고 _____

C 의미가 같도록 알맞은 단어를 넣어 문장을 완성하세요.

1. I can't _____ over 50,000 won on it.
   나는 그것에 5만원 이상 쓸 수 없어.

2. I can't _____ one, either.
   나도 표를 살 돈이 안돼.

3. It says they are picking new _____.
   새로운 모델을 뽑고 있다고 하네.

4. Yes, let's get her to _____ on this skateboard.
   그래, 브라우니가 이 스케이트보드 위에 포즈를 취하게 하자.

5. Good. I'll take her _____.
   좋아, 내가 사진을 찍을게.

6. Ugh! Brownie _____ standing on the skateboard.
   어! 브라우니는 스케이트보드 위에 서 있는 것을 몹시 싫어해.

7. Calm down, Brownie. I don't want to _____ you.
   진정해, 브라우니. 너를 화나게 하고 싶지 않아.

8. Here, have some tuna as a _____.
   자 여기, 상으로 참치 좀 먹어.

D 녹음된 내용을 듣고, 다음 빈칸에 들어갈 단어나 표현을 쓰세요. 🎧

Bomi: I can't buy a _____ to the Volcanoes' _____. ● I can't
_____ over 50,000 won on it.

Sara: I can't _____ one, either. ● They are so _____!

Bomi: Hey, look at that _____ . ● That dog is riding a _____.

Sara: It says they are picking new _____. ● The winners get _____
money. ● We should _____ Brownie!

Bomi: Yes, let's get her to _____ on this skateboard.

Sara: Put these _____ on her. ● Good. I'll take her _____.

Bomi: Ugh! Brownie _____ _____ on the skateboard. ● Calm
down, Brownie. ● I don't want to _____ you. ● I'm _____
you, Brownie!

Sara: Yes, I finally got it! ● _____, Brownie!

Bomi: Great, we _____! ● Good _____, Brownie!

Sara: Here, have some tuna as a _____.

Bomi: Have some milk, Brownie. ● You look _____.

Chapter 4 Economy

▶ 1단계 : 먼저 그림을 보고, 이 장의 에피소드를 추측해 보세요.

→ take a deep breath

catch everyone's attention ←

→ can't find a thief

fit someone perfectly ←

Dear Seri,

You look so cute today, Seri. ● You're such a warm-hearted person. ● Please take a deep breath and listen to me. ● You know your brand-new MP3 player? ● Well, I borrowed it and took it to school. ● It caught everyone's attention. ● My classmates thought it was really cool. ● But when I returned from PE class it wasn't in my bag. ● Someone stole it! ● We couldn't find the thief. ● Oh, I should have listened to mom's advice. ● She said I should leave it at home. ● Look, my favorite jacket is yours. ● It will fit you perfectly. ● It was a bit tight for me anyway. ● It's a really famous brand. ● It's perfect except that it's two years old. ● So take it and please forgive me!

▶ 3단계 : 외우면서 단어를 2번씩 써보세요!

1 cute [kjúːt]
a. 귀여운, 예쁜

_____   _____

2 warm-hearted [wɔ́ːrmháːrtid]
a. 인정이 있는, 친절한

_____   _____

3 deep [díːp]
a. 깊은
▶ depth n. 깊이

_____   _____

4 breath [bréθ]
n. 숨, 호흡
▶ breathe v. 숨쉬다
▶ take a breath 숨을 쉬다

_____   _____

5 brand-new [brǽndnjùː]
a. 아주 새로운, 신품의

_____   _____

6 borrow [bɔ́(ː)rou | bár-]
v. 빌리다
▶ lend v. 빌려주다

_____   _____

7 attention [əténʃən]
n. 주의, 주목
▶ attentive a. 주의 깊은, 경청하는
▶ catch one's attention ~의 주의를 끌다

_____   _____

8 cool [kúːl]
a. 멋진, 시원한

_____   _____

9 return [ritə́ːrn]
v. 되돌아오다(가다)
▶ return - returned - returned

_____   _____

10 steal [stíːl]
v. 훔치다
▶ stolen a. 훔친
▶ steal - stole - stolen

_____   _____

11 thief [θíːf]
n. 도둑

_____   _____

▶ 외우면서 단어를 2번씩 써보세요!

12 **advice** [ədváis]
n. 조언, 충고
▶ advise v. 조언하다

_____ _____

13 **leave** [líːv]
v. 남기다, 두고 가다(오다)
▶ leave - left - left

_____ _____

14 **favorite** [féivərit]
a. 좋아하는

_____ _____

15 **fit** [fít]
v. ~에 꼭 맞다, 어울리다
▶ fitness n. 적합, 적성, 건강함
▶ fit - fitted - fitted

_____ _____

16 **bit** [bít]
n. 조각, 조금
▶ a bit n. 조금, 약간

_____ _____

17 **tight** [táit]
a. 꼭 끼는
▶ tighten v. 죄다, 조이다

_____ _____

18 **anyway** [éniwèi]
ad. 어쨌든, 아무튼

_____ _____

19 **famous** [féiməs]
a. 유명한
▶ fame n. 명성

_____ _____

20 **except** [iksépt]
conj. ~를 제외하고
prep. ~외에는
▶ exception n. 예외

_____ _____

21 **forgive** [fərgív]
v. 용서하다
▶ forgiveness n. 용서, 관용
▶ forgive - forgave – forgiven

_____ _____

Exercise

A 다음 주어진 단어의 우리말 뜻을 쓰세요.

① warm-hearted _____　② brand-new _____
③ attention _____　④ cool _____
⑤ return _____　⑥ advice _____
⑦ leave _____　⑧ fit _____
⑨ anyway _____　⑩ except _____

B 다음 우리말 뜻에 해당하는 영어 단어를 쓰세요.

① 깊은 _____
② 숨, 호흡 _____
③ 빌리다 _____
④ 훔치다 _____
⑤ 도둑 _____
⑥ 좋아하는 _____
⑦ 조금, 조각 _____
⑧ 꼭 끼는 _____
⑨ 유명한 _____
⑩ 용서하다 _____

C 의미가 같도록 알맞은 단어를 넣어 문장을 완성하세요.

1. You look so _____ today, Seri.
   너 오늘 정말 귀엽다, 세리.

2. Please take a _____ breath and listen to me.
   제발 숨을 크게 쉬고 내 말을 좀 들어줘.

3. It caught everyone's _____.
   모든 애들의 시선을 사로잡았어.

4. But when I _____ from PE class it wasn't in my bag.
   그런데 체육 시간이 끝나고 돌아오니 그것이 내 가방 안에 없었어.

5. Oh, I should have listened to mom's _____.
   아, 나는 엄마의 조언을 들었어야 했어.

6. It was a _____ tight for me _____.
   어차피 나에게는 조금 끼었거든.

7. It's perfect _____ that it's two years old.
   2년 정도 되었다는 것을 제외하면 완벽해.

8. So take it and please _____ me!
   그러니 그것을 갖고 제발 나를 용서해 줘!

D 녹음된 내용을 듣고, 다음 빈칸에 들어갈 단어나 표현을 쓰세요. 🎧

Dear Seri,

You look so _____ today, Seri. ● You're such a _____ person.
● Please take a _____ _____ and listen to me. ● You know your
_____ MP3 player? ● Well, I _____ it and took it to
_____. ● It caught everyone's attention. ● My classmates thought it was
really _____. ● But when I _____ from PE class it wasn't in
my bag. ● Someone _____ it! ● We couldn't find the _____. ● Oh, I
should have listened to mom's _____. ● She said I should _____
it at home. ● Look, my _____ jacket is yours. ● It will _____
you perfectly. ● It was a _____ _____ for me _____. ● It's a really
_____ brand. ● It's perfect _____ that it's two years old. ● So take
it and please _____ me!

■ 녹음을 듣고, 해당하는 단어와 뜻을 쓰세요.

1	단어:	뜻:	2	단어:	뜻:
3	단어:	뜻:	4	단어:	뜻:
5	단어:	뜻:	6	단어:	뜻:
7	단어:	뜻:	8	단어:	뜻:
9	단어:	뜻:	10	단어:	뜻:
11	단어:	뜻:	12	단어:	뜻:
13	단어:	뜻:	14	단어:	뜻:
15	단어:	뜻:	16	단어:	뜻:
17	단어:	뜻:	18	단어:	뜻:
19	단어:	뜻:	20	단어:	뜻:
21	단어:	뜻:	22	단어:	뜻:
23	단어:	뜻:	24	단어:	뜻:
25	단어:	뜻:	26	단어:	뜻:
27	단어:	뜻:	28	단어:	뜻:
29	단어:	뜻:	30	단어:	뜻:

Voca Plus

At a supermarket

1. **cashier** 출납계원
2. **shopper** 쇼핑하는 사람
3. **counter** 계산대
4. **credit card** 신용카드
5. **shopping list** 쇼핑 리스트
6. **shopping cart** 쇼핑 카트
7. **express lane** 빠른 계산대
8. **receipt** 영수증
9. **parcel** 꾸러미

Culture Plus

At a bank 은행에서

+ **bank book** 통장
+ **credit card** 신용카드
+ **ATM** 현금 자동 인출기
+ **bank teller** 은행 직원
+ **cash** 현금
+ **coin** 동전

+ **bill** 지폐
+ **check** 수표

SMART

Level.2

VOCA EDGE

Chapter 5 Technology

▶ 1단계 : 먼저 그림을 보고, 이 장의 에피소드를 추측해 보세요.

→ bend one's legs

serve food ←

→ invite friends over

Dear Diary,

Sara and I left to go downtown. ● Now, we are at the robot contest. ● Wow, robots can do plenty of things. ● Some robots even carry furniture.

S a r a : Look at that robot. ● It's greeting people! ● It can bend its legs.

Bomi: I like its gentle smile.

S a r a : The robot is counting sheets of paper.

Bomi: Hey, the robot over there is serving food. ● And the robot beside it is mixing something. ● I can see it mixing flour and eggs.

S a r a : It looks more like a human than a machine. ● The inventors must be geniuses.

Bomi: I want to have a compact robot. ● I don't want it to be heavy. ● I will invite friends over more often if it helps me with cleaning.

S a r a : The robot has to be clever. ● I want it to drive us to school.

1 **downtown** [dáuntáun]
ad. 도심지로
n. 시내, 도심지

_____   _____

2 **contest** [kántest / kɔ́n-]
n. 대회, 경연, 콘테스트

_____   _____

3 **plenty** [plénti]
n. 많음 a. 많은
▶ plentiful a. 많은
▶ plenty of 많은

_____   _____

4 **thing** [θíŋ]
n. 물건, 것

_____   _____

5 **carry** [kǽri]
v. 나르다, 운반하다
▶ carry - carried - carried

_____   _____

6 **furniture** [fɔ́:rnitʃər]
n. 가구

_____   _____

7 **greet** [grí:t]
v. 인사하다
▶ greeting n. 인사
▶ greet - greeted- greeted

_____   _____

8 **bend** [bénd]
v. 구부리다
▶ bendable a. 구부릴 수 있는
▶ bend - bent - bent

_____   _____

9 **smile** [smail]]
n. 미소 v. 미소 짓다
▶ smiling a. 미소 짓는

_____   _____

10 **sheet** [ʃí:t]
n. 한 장, 시트

_____   _____

▶ 외우면서 단어를 2번씩 써보세요!

11 serve [sə́:rv]
v. 음식을 내다, 음식 시중을 들다
▶ service n. 봉사
▶ serve - served - served

_____   _____

12 mix [míks]
v. 혼합하다, 섞다
▶ mixture n. 혼합
▶ mix - mixed - mixed

_____   _____

13 flour [fláuər]
n. 밀가루

_____   _____

14 machine [məʃíːn]
n. 기계

_____   _____

15 genius [dʒíːnjəs]
n. 천재

_____   _____

16 compact [kəmpǽkt]
a. 아담한

_____   _____

17 heavy [hévi]
a. 무거운
▶ heavily ad. 무겁게

_____   _____

18 invite [inváit]
v. 초대하다
▶ invitation n. 초대
▶ invite - invited - invited

_____   _____

19 often [ɔ́(:)ftən]
ad. 자주, 종종

_____   _____

20 clever [klévər]
a. 영리한, 똑똑한

_____   _____

21 drive [dràiv]
v. 운전하다 n. 드라이브
▶ driver n. 운전사
▶ drive - drove – driven

_____   _____

Exercise

A 다음 주어진 단어의 우리말 뜻을 쓰세요.

① downtown ＿＿＿＿＿＿ ② contest ＿＿＿＿＿＿

③ plenty ＿＿＿＿＿＿ ④ carry ＿＿＿＿＿＿

⑤ serve ＿＿＿＿＿＿ ⑥ mix ＿＿＿＿＿＿

⑦ often ＿＿＿＿＿＿ ⑧ clever ＿＿＿＿＿＿

⑨ drive ＿＿＿＿＿＿ ⑩ greet ＿＿＿＿＿＿

B 다음 우리말 뜻에 해당하는 영어 단어를 쓰세요.

① 물건, 것 ＿＿＿＿＿＿＿＿＿＿

② 가구 ＿＿＿＿＿＿＿＿＿＿

③ 구부리다 ＿＿＿＿＿＿＿＿＿＿

④ 한 장, 시트 ＿＿＿＿＿＿＿＿＿＿

⑤ 밀가루 ＿＿＿＿＿＿＿＿＿＿

⑥ 기계 ＿＿＿＿＿＿＿＿＿＿

⑦ 천재 ＿＿＿＿＿＿＿＿＿＿

⑧ 아담한 ＿＿＿＿＿＿＿＿＿＿

⑨ 무거운 ＿＿＿＿＿＿＿＿＿＿

⑩ 초대하다 ＿＿＿＿＿＿＿＿＿＿

C 의미가 같도록 알맞은 단어를 넣어 문장을 완성하세요.

1. Wow, robots can do ＿＿＿＿＿ of things.
와, 로봇은 많은 것들을 할 수 있어.

2. Some robots even ＿＿＿＿＿ furniture.
몇몇 로봇들은 심지어 가구도 운반할 수 있어.

3. Look at that robot. It's ＿＿＿＿＿ people!
저 로봇 봐. 사람들에게 인사하고 있어!

4. Hey, the robot over there is ＿＿＿＿＿ food.
이봐, 저기 있는 로봇은 음식을 내고 있어.

5. It looks more like a human than a ＿＿＿＿＿.
기계보다는 사람처럼 생겼어.

6. The inventors must be ＿＿＿＿＿.
그 발명가들은 천재들임에 틀림이 없어.

7. I will ＿＿＿＿＿ friends over more often if it helps me with cleaning.
그것이 청소를 도와준다면 나는 친구들을 더 자주 초대할 거야.

8. The robot has to be ＿＿＿＿＿.
그 로봇은 똑똑해야겠네.

D 녹음된 내용을 듣고, 다음 빈칸에 들어갈 단어나 표현을 쓰세요. 🎧

Dear Diary,

Sara and I left to go _____. ● Now, we are at the robot _____. ● Wow, robots can do _____ of _____. ● Some robots even _____ _____.

. . . .

Sara: Look at that robot. ● It's _____ people! ● It can _____ its legs.

Bomi: I like its gentle _____.

Sara: The robot is counting sheets of _____.

Bomi: Hey, the robot over there is _____ food. ● And the robot beside it is _____ something. ● I can see it mixing _____ and eggs.

Sara: It looks more like a human than a _____. ● The inventors must be _____.

Bomi: I want to have a _____ robot. ● I don't want it to be _____. ● I will _____ friends over more _____ if it helps me with cleaning.

Sara: The robot has to be _____. ● I want it to _____ us to school.

▶ 1단계 : 먼저 그림을 보고, 이 장의 에피소드를 추측해 보세요.

→ **enjoy modern technology**

cheer someone up ←

→ **take pictures with a cell phone**

go fishing on an island ←

Dear Diary,

My grandma really enjoys modern technology. ● Last year mom couldn't attend my graduation. ● So grandma tried to cheer me up. ● She said "Cheese" and took pictures of me during the ceremony.

Grandma: Bomi, it's really convenient to take pictures with my cell phone.

B o m i : It's wonderful that you enjoy modern culture.

Grandma: I want to rent a computer. ● I can't send messages to my community members.

B o m i : Grandma, what's the matter with your computer?

Grandma: I called a repair person because it's broken.

B o m i : You can use a computer at the library. ● By the way, grandma, you're becoming more sociable. ● Do you belong to the Internet fishing community?

Grandma: Yeah, I joined it last month. ● You know, grandpa and Ilike fishing.

B o m i : Then, you're a member of the fishing community. ● Do you get a lot of information about fishing?

Grandma: Sure. Grandpa and I are going to go fishing on an island next month with the members.

B o m i : You two are full of energy.

▶ 3단계 : 외우면서 단어를 2번씩 써보세요!

1 **modern** [mάdərn]
a. 현대의

_____ _____

2 **technology** [teknάlədʒi]
n. 기술

_____ _____

3 **graduation** [græʤuéiʃən]
n. 졸업
▶ graduate v. 졸업하다

_____ _____

4 **cheer** [tʃíər]
v. 격려하다
n. 격려, 환호
▶ cheerful a. 쾌활한, 기분 좋은
▶ cheer up 기운이 나게 하다, 기분 좋게 하다
▶ cheer - cheered - cheered

_____ _____

5 **picture** [píktʃər]
n. 사진
▶ take a picture 사진을 찍다

_____ _____

6 **ceremony** [sérəmòuni]
n. 식, 의식

_____ _____

7 **convenient** [kənví:njənt]
a. 편리한
▶ convenience n. 편리함

_____ _____

8 **culture** [kʌ́ltʃər]
n. 문명, 문화
▶ cultural a. 문화의

_____ _____

9 **rent** [rént]
v. 대여하다
n. 집세, 임대료
▶ rent - rented - rented

_____ _____

10 **member** [mémbər]
n. 회원, 일원

_____ _____

▶ 외우면서 단어를 2번씩 써보세요!

⑪ matter [mǽtər]
n. 문제, 중요성 v. 문제가 되다, 중요하다

_____   _____

⑫ repair [ripέər]
n. 수리, 수선 v. 수리하다
▶ repairable a. 수리 가능한

_____   _____

⑬ library [láibrèri]
n. 도서관

_____   _____

⑭ sociable [sóuʃəbəl]
a. 사교성 있는
▶ society n. 사회, 사교
▶ social a. 사회적인

_____   _____

⑮ belong [bilɔ́(:)ŋ]
v. ~에 속하다, 소속하다
▶ belonging n. 소유물
▶ belong to ~에 속하다
▶ belong - belonged - belonged

_____   _____

⑯ join [dʒɔ́in]
v. 가입하다
▶ join - joined - joined

_____   _____

⑰ last [lǽːst]
a. 지난, 마지막의

_____   _____

⑱ fishing [fíʃiŋ]
n. 낚시
▶ fish v. 낚시하다

_____   _____

⑲ information [ìnfərméiʃən]
n. 정보
▶ inform v. 정보를 제공하다

_____   _____

⑳ island [áilənd]
n. 섬

_____   _____

㉑ full [fúl]
a. 가득 찬
▶ be full of ~로 가득차다

_____   _____

Exercise

A 다음 주어진 단어의 우리말 뜻을 쓰세요.

① modern _____   ② cheer _____

③ ceremony _____   ④ rent _____

⑤ matter _____   ⑥ repair _____

⑦ belong _____   ⑧ last _____

⑨ full _____   ⑩ graduation _____

B 다음 우리말 뜻에 해당하는 영어 단어를 쓰세요.

① 기술 _____

② 편리한 _____

③ 문명, 문화 _____

④ 회원, 일원 _____

⑤ 도서관 _____

⑥ 사교성 있는 _____

⑦ 가입하다 _____

⑧ 정보 _____

⑨ 섬 _____

⑩ 사진 _____

C 의미가 같도록 알맞은 단어를 넣어 문장을 완성하세요.

1. My grandma really enjoys _____ technology.
   우리 할머니는 정말로 현대 기술을 즐기셔.

2. Last year mom couldn't attend my _____.
   작년에 엄마가 나의 졸업식에 참석하지 못하셨어.

3. Bomi, it's really _____ to take pictures with my cell phone.
   보미, 내 휴대 전화로 사진 찍는 것이 정말 편리하구나.

4. I called a _____ person because it's broken.
   그것이 고장이 나서 정비사를 불렀어.

5. By the way, grandma, you're becoming more _____.
   그런데, 할머니, 점점 더 사교적으로 변하시네요.

6. Do you _____ to the Internet fishing community?
   인터넷 낚시 동호회 소속이세요?

7. You know, grandpa and I like _____.
   너도 알다시피, 할아버지와 나는 낚시를 좋아해.

8. Do you get a lot of _____ about fishing?
   낚시에 관한 정보도 많이 얻나요?

D 녹음된 내용을 듣고, 다음 빈칸에 들어갈 단어나 표현을 쓰세요. 🎧

Dear Diary,

My grandma really enjoys _____ _____. ● Last year mom couldn't attend my _____. ● So grandma tried to _____ me up. ● She said "Cheese" and took _____ of me during the _____.

Grandma: Bomi, it's really _____ to take pictures with my cell phone.

B o m i : It's wonderful that you enjoy modern _____.

Grandma: I want to _____ a computer. ● I can't send messages to my community _____.

B o m i : Grandma, what's the _____ with your computer?

Grandma: I called a _____ person because it's broken.

B o m i : You can use a computer at the _____. ● By the way, grandma, you're becoming more _____. ● Do you _____ to the Internet fishing community?

Grandma: Yeah, I _____ it _____ month. ● You know, grandpa and I like _____.

B o m i : Then, you're a member of the fishing community. ● Do you get a lot of _____ about fishing?

Grandma: Sure. Grandpa and I are going to go fishing on an _____ next month with the members.

B o m i : You two are _____ of energy.

■ 녹음을 듣고, 해당하는 단어와 뜻을 쓰세요.

1	단어:	뜻:	2	단어:	뜻:
3	단어:	뜻:	4	단어:	뜻:
5	단어:	뜻:	6	단어:	뜻:
7	단어:	뜻:	8	단어:	뜻:
9	단어:	뜻:	10	단어:	뜻:
11	단어:	뜻:	12	단어:	뜻:
13	단어:	뜻:	14	단어:	뜻:
15	단어:	뜻:	16	단어:	뜻:
17	단어:	뜻:	18	단어:	뜻:
19	단어:	뜻:	20	단어:	뜻:
21	단어:	뜻:	22	단어:	뜻:
23	단어:	뜻:	24	단어:	뜻:
25	단어:	뜻:	26	단어:	뜻:
27	단어:	뜻:	28	단어:	뜻:
29	단어:	뜻:	30	단어:	뜻:

Voca Plus

Household appliances

1. **blender** 블렌더
2. **toaster** 토스터
3. **microwave** 전자레인지
4. **vacuum cleaner** 청소기
5. **washing machine** 세탁기
6. **iron** 다리미
7. **laptop** 노트북 컴퓨터
8. **coffee machine** 커피 머신
9. **refrigerator** 냉장고
10. **cassette tape recorder**
    카세트 테이프 레코더

Culture Plus

In a lab 실험실에서

+ **alcohol lamp** 알코올램프   + **material** 물질, 재료

+ **test tube** 시험관   + **solid** 고체

+ **thermometer** 온도계   + **liquid** 액체

+ **solution** 용액   + **gas** 기체

+ **measuring flask** 플라스크

+ **filter paper** 거름종이

SMART

Level.2

VOCA EDGE

Chapter 6

Nature and Space

▶ 1단계 : 먼저 그림을 보고, 이 장의 에피소드를 추측해 보세요.

→ **talk about pollution**

use old jeans and make a wallet ←

→ **make soap out of used oil**

sprout from the bottles ←

Bomi: We discussed an interesting topic in class. ● We talked about pollution.

Sara: That's a huge global issue these days.

Bomi: The environment is so important. ● It affects us all the time. ● And it treats us all the same. ● We are all equally affected. ● One thing everyone can do is to reduce the amount of garbage we produce.

Sara: Yes, we can reuse things. ● Take a look at my new wallet. ● I used my old jeans to make it.

Bomi: Were they out of fashion?

Sara: Yes, but now they are still being useful as a wallet!

Bomi: My mom makes our soap. ● She makes it out of used cooking oil!

Sara: My mom reuses empty plastic bottles. ● She grows plants in them. ● I sometimes help her put in the flower seeds. ● Soon flowers will sprout from the bottles!

▶ 3단계 : 외우면서 단어를 2번씩 써보세요!

① discuss [diskʌ́s]
v. 토론하다, 논의하다
▶ discussion n. 토론, 토의

_____   _____

② topic [tápik / tɔ́p-]
n. 논제, 주제

_____   _____

③ pollution [pəlúːʃən]
n. 공해, 오염
▶ pollute v. 오염시키다
▶ polluted a. 오염된

_____   _____

④ global [glóubəl]
a. 세계적인, 전 세계의
▶ globe n. 지구

_____   _____

⑤ environment [inváiərənmənt]
n. 환경
▶ environmental a. 환경의, 주위의

_____   _____

⑥ affect [əfékt]
v. ~에 영향을 미치다 n. 영향
▶ affect - affected - affected

_____   _____

⑦ treat [tríːt]
v. 대우하다, 취급하다
▶ treat - treated - treated

_____   _____

⑧ equally [íːkwəli]
ad. 똑같게, 균등하게
▶ equal a. 같은, 동등한

_____   _____

⑨ reduce [ridʒúːs]
v. 줄이다
▶ reduction n. 감소, 하락
▶ reduce - reduced - reduced

_____   _____

⑩ reuse [riːjúːz]
v. 다시 사용하다 n. 재사용
▶ use v. 사용하다
▶ reusable a. 재사용할 수 있는
▶ reused a. 재생한

_____   _____

▶ 외우면서 단어를 2번씩 써보세요!

⑪ wallet [wɔ́lit / wɔ́l-]
n. 지갑

_____   _____

⑫ jeans [dʒíːnz]
n. 청바지

_____   _____

⑬ fashion [fǽʃən]
n. 유행, 패션
▶ out of fashion 유행이 지난
▶ in fashion 유행하고 있는

_____   _____

⑭ useful [júːsfəl]
a. 유용한
▶ useless a. 쓸모없는, 무익한

_____   _____

⑮ soap [sóup]
n. 비누

_____   _____

⑯ cooking oil [kúkiŋ ɔ́il]
식용유

_____   _____

⑰ empty [émpti]
a. 텅 빈

_____   _____

⑱ grow [gróu]
v. 기르다, 재배하다
▶ growth n. 성장, 재배, 배양
▶ grow - grew - grown

_____   _____

⑲ seed [síːd]
n. 씨앗 v. 씨를 뿌리다

_____   _____

⑳ sprout [spraut]
v. 싹트다, 나기 시작하다
n. 싹
▶ sprout - sprouted - sprouted

_____   _____

㉑ bottle [bátl]
n. 병

_____   _____

Exercise

A 다음 주어진 단어의 우리말 뜻을 쓰세요.

① discuss _____   ② global _____
③ affect _____   ④ equally _____
⑤ reuse _____   ⑥ grow _____
⑦ seed _____   ⑧ sprout _____
⑨ pollution _____   ⑩ treat _____

B 다음 우리말 뜻에 해당하는 영어 단어를 쓰세요.

① 논제, 주제 _____
② 환경 _____
③ 줄이다 _____
④ 지갑 _____
⑤ 청바지 _____
⑥ 유용한 _____
⑦ 비누 _____
⑧ 식용유 _____
⑨ 텅 빈 _____
⑩ 병 _____

C 의미가 같도록 알맞은 단어를 넣어 문장을 완성하세요.

1. We _____ an interesting topic in class.
   우리는 수업시간에 재미있는 주제를 토론했어.

2. The _____ is so important.
   환경은 아주 중요해.

3. And it _____ us all the same.
   그리고 환경은 우리 모두를 똑같이 취급해.

4. One thing everyone can do is to _____ the amount of garbage we produce.
   모든 사람이 할 수 있는 건 우리가 배출하는 쓰레기의 양을 줄이는 거야.

5. Take a look at my new _____.
   내 새로운 지갑을 좀 봐.

6. Were they out of _____?
   유행이 지난 거였니?

7. She makes it out of used _____!
   사용한 식용유로 비누를 만드시는 거야.

8. Soon flowers will _____ from the bottles!
   곧 병에서 꽃들이 나기 시작할 거야.

D 녹음된 내용을 듣고, 다음 빈칸에 들어갈 단어나 표현을 쓰세요. 🎧

Bomi: We _____ an interesting _____ in class. ● We talked about _____.

Sara: That's a huge _____ issue these days.

Bomi: The _____ is so important. ● It _____ us all the time. ● And it _____ us all the same. ● We are all _____ affected. ● One thing everyone can do is to _____ the amount of garbage we produce.

Sara: Yes, we can _____ things. ● Take a look at my new _____. ● I used my old _____ to make it.

Bomi: Were they out of fashion?

Sara: Yes, but now they are still being _____ as a wallet!

Bomi: My mom makes our _____. ● She makes it out of used _____!

Sara: My mom reuses _____ plastic bottles. ● She _____ plants in them. ● I sometimes help her put in the flower _____. ● Soon flowers will _____ from the _____!

▶ 1단계 : 먼저 그림을 보고, 이 장의 에피소드를 추측해 보세요.

→ look at an interesting article

go on a balloon ride ←

→ pilot the balloon

land safely on the ground ←

Episode

Dear Diary,

Dad and I are looking at an interesting article in the papers. ● It's about leisure activities. ● There will be a hot-air balloon festival tomorrow. ● We're thinking of going on a balloon ride. ● We can enjoy the beautiful scenery all around. ● It will be good for the mind and body.

The article says there is a balloonist. ● He pilots the balloon. ● It's filled with gas. ● The balloonist sometimes lets you help inflate the balloon! ● After the balloon starts its flight, the balloonist controls it and follows a set course. ● About an hour later, he will land it safely on the ground. ● Hot-air balloons are usually safe from accidents. ● And tomorrow's weather forecast is very good. ● It says the wind will be mild. ● What does this mean? ● Perfect weather for a balloon ride!

▶ 3단계 : 외우면서 단어를 2번씩 써보세요!

1 **article** [ɑ́:rtikl]
n. 기사, 논설

2 **paper** [péipər]
n. 신문, 종이

3 **leisure** [líːʒər]
n. 여가, 자유시간

4 **activity** [æktívəti]
n. 활동, 운동

5 **hot-air balloon**
[hɑ́tɛ́ər bəlúːn]
열기구

6 **balloon ride** [bəlúːn raid]
열기구 타기

7 **scenery** [síːnəri]
n. 풍경

8 **mind** [máind]
n. 마음, 정신

9 **balloonist** [bəlúːnist]
n. 열기구 비행사

10 **pilot** [páilət]
v. 조정하다
▶ pilot - piloted - piloted

11 **fill** [fíl]
v. 채우다
▶ be filled with ~으로 채워지다
▶ fill - filled - filled

▶ 외우면서 단어를 2번씩 써보세요!

⑫ **inflate** [infléit]
v. (풍선 등을) 부풀게 하다
▶ inflation n. 팽창, 부풀리기
▶ inflate - inflated - inflated

_____ _____

⑬ **control** [kəntróul]
v. 통제하다
▶ control - controlled - controlled

_____ _____

⑭ **course** [kɔ́ːrs]
n. 경로, 진로

_____ _____

⑮ **land** [lǽnd]
v. 착륙시키다, 착륙하다
n. 땅, 육지
▶ land - landed - landed

_____ _____

⑯ **accident** [ǽksidənt]
n. 사고

_____ _____

⑰ **forecast** [fɔ́ːrkæ̀stl]
n. 예보, 예상 v. 예보하다

_____ _____

⑱ **wind** [wínd]
n. 바람
▶ windy a. 바람 부는, 심한

_____ _____

⑲ **mild** [máild]
a. 온화한, 순한

_____ _____

⑳ **mean** [míːn]
v. 의미하다
▶ meaning n. 의미
▶ mean - meant - meant

_____ _____

㉑ **perfect** [pə́ːrfikt]
a. 완벽한 v. 완성하다
▶ perfection n. 완전, 완벽

_____ _____

Exercise

A 다음 주어진 단어의 우리말 뜻을 쓰세요.

① article   _____   ② leisure   _____

③ balloon ride _____   ④ inflate   _____

⑤ course   _____   ⑥ land   _____

⑦ forecast   _____   ⑧ mild   _____

⑨ perfect   _____   ⑩ activity   _____

B 다음 우리말 뜻에 해당하는 영어 단어를 쓰세요.

① 신문, 종이   _____

② 열기구   _____

③ 풍경   _____

④ 마음, 정신   _____

⑤ 열기구 비행사   _____

⑥ 조정하다   _____

⑦ 통제하다   _____

⑧ 사고   _____

⑨ 의미하다   _____

⑩ 채우다   _____

C 의미가 같도록 알맞은 단어를 넣어 문장을 완성하세요.

1. Dad and I are looking at an interesting _____ in the papers.
아빠와 나는 신문에서 재미있는 기사를 살펴보고 있어.

2. It's about _____ activities.
그것은 여가 활동에 관한 거야.

3. We can enjoy the beautiful _____ all around.
사방의 아름다운 풍경을 감상할 수 있어.

4. He _____ the balloon.
그는 열기구를 조정해.

5. The balloonist sometimes lets you help _____ the balloon!
가끔 비행사가 열기구를 부풀리는 일을 도와주게 해준대!

6. About an hour later, he will _____ it safely on the ground.
한 시간쯤 후에 그는 안전하게 땅 위로 열기구를 착륙시킬 거야.

7. And tomorrow's weather _____ is very good.
게다가 내일 일기예보가 아주 좋아.

8. It says the _____ will be mild.
내일 바람이 약할 거래.

D 녹음된 내용을 듣고, 다음 빈칸에 들어갈 단어나 표현을 쓰세요. 🎧

Dear Diary,

Dad and I are looking at an interesting _____ in the _____. ● It's about _____ _____. ● There will be a _____ festival _____. ● We're thinking of going on a balloon ride. ● We can enjoy the beautiful _____ all around. ● It will be good for the _____ and body.

The article says there is a _____. ● He _____ the balloon. ● It's _____ with gas. ● The balloonist sometimes lets you help _____ the balloon! ● After the balloon starts its flight, the balloonist _____ it and follows a set _____. ● About an hour later, he will _____ it safely on the ground. ● Hot-air balloons are usually safe from _____. ● And tomorrow's weather _____ is very good. ● It says the _____ will be _____. ● What does this _____? ● _____ weather for a balloon ride!

▶ 1단계 : 먼저 그림을 보고, 이 장의 에피소드를 추측해 보세요.

→ be about to go out

blow up a balloon ←

→ make hair stand up straight

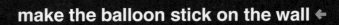
make the balloon stick on the wall ←

Dear Diary,

Hoony and I were about to go out. ● But suddenly, it started to rain. ● We could hear thunder, too. ● Hoony wanted to do an experiment. ● "I'll be the leader," he said. ● First, Hoony blew up a balloon. ● "Rub this on your head," he said. ● The balloon made my hair stand up straight! ● Then Hoony made the balloon stick on the wall! ● "What's the secret?" I asked. ● "The balloon has static electricity," Hoony said. ● "It's okay to touch it. ● Static electricity isn't dangerous," Hoony explained. ● "You can use static electricity to make a lemon battery." ● "We just need a lemon and a few tools," Hoony said.

It was very strange. ● Hoony's brain was very active today. ● He was like a real scientist.

It's interesting that a lemon can be used as a medium to create electricity.

▶ 3단계 : 외우면서 단어를 2번씩 써보세요!

① **be about to** [biː əbáut tuː]
지금 막 ~하려고 하다

_____ _____

② **suddenly** [sʌ́dnli]
ad. 갑자기
▶ sudden a. 갑작스러운, 뜻밖의

_____ _____

③ **hear** [híər]
v. 듣다, 들리다
▶ hear - heard - heard

_____ _____

④ **thunder** [θʌ́ndər]
n. 천둥

_____ _____

⑤ **experiment** [ikspérəmənt]
n. 실험 v. 실험하다

_____ _____

⑥ **leader** [líːdər]
n. 지도자, 리더

_____ _____

⑦ **blow** [blóu]
v. 불다
▶ blow up 부풀리다
▶ blow - blew - blown

_____ _____

⑧ **hair** [hέər]
n. 머리카락

_____ _____

⑨ **straight** [stréit]
a. 곧은, 똑바로 선

_____ _____

⑩ **stick** [stík]
v. 붙이다, 찌르다
▶ stick - stuck - stuck

_____ _____

⑪ **secret** [síːkrit]
n. 비밀

_____ _____

⑫ **static** [stǽtik]
a. 정적인, 정전기의

_____ _____

▶ 외우면서 단어를 2번씩 써보세요!

⑬ **touch** [tʌtʃ]
v. 만지다, 건드리다
n. 만짐, 촉감
▶ touch - touched - touched

_____ _____

⑭ **dangerous** [déindʒərəs]
a. 위험한
▶ danger n. 위험
▶ dangerously ad. 위험하게

_____ _____

⑮ **explain** [ikspléin]
v. 설명하다
▶ explanation n. 설명
▶ explain - explained - explained

_____ _____

⑯ **battery** [bǽtəri]
n. 전지, 배터리

_____ _____

⑰ **tool** [túːl]
n. 도구, 연장

_____ _____

⑱ **strange** [stréindʒ]
a. 이상한, 묘한
▶ strangely ad. 이상하게

_____ _____

⑲ **active** [ǽktiv]
a. 활동적인, 활발한
▶ activeness n. 활발함, 적극성

_____ _____

⑳ **scientist** [sáiəntist]
n. 과학자
▶ science n. 과학
▶ scientific a. 과학의, 과학적인

_____ _____

㉑ **medium** [míːdiəm]
n. 매체, 매개물

_____ _____

Exercise

A 다음 주어진 단어의 우리말 뜻을 쓰세요.

① be about to _____   ② experiment _____

③ hear _____   ④ straight _____

⑤ stick _____   ⑥ touch _____

⑦ static _____   ⑧ strange _____

⑨ active _____   ⑩ medium _____

B 다음 우리말 뜻에 해당하는 영어 단어를 쓰세요.

① 갑자기 _____

② 천둥 _____

③ 불다 _____

④ 머리카락 _____

⑤ 비밀 _____

⑥ 위험한 _____

⑦ 설명하다 _____

⑧ 전지, 배터리 _____

⑨ 도구, 연장 _____

⑩ 과학자 _____

C 의미가 같도록 알맞은 단어를 넣어 문장을 완성하세요.

1. Hoony and I _____ go out.
   후니와 나는 막 나가려는 참이었어.

2. Hoony wanted to do an _____.
   후니는 실험을 하고 싶어했어.

3. "I'll be the _____," he said.
   "내가 리더를 할래." 그가 말했어.

4. The balloon made my _____ stand up straight!
   풍선이 내 머리카락을 곧게 서도록 만들었어!

5. Then Hoony made the balloon _____ on the wall!
   그리고 후니는 풍선을 벽에 붙게 했어!

6. "It's okay to touch it. Static electricity isn't _____," Hoony explained.
   "그것을 만져도 괜찮아. 정전기는 위험하지 않아." 후니가 설명했어.

7. You can use _____ electricity to make a lemon battery.
   정전기를 이용해서 레몬 전지를 만들 수 있어.

8. He was like a real _____.
   그는 진짜 과학자 같았어.

D 녹음된 내용을 듣고, 다음 빈칸에 들어갈 단어나 표현을 쓰세요.

Dear Diary,

Hoony and I _____ go out. ● But _____, it started to rain. ● We could _____ _____, too. ● Hoony wanted to do an experiment. ● "I'll be the _____," he said. ● First, Hoony _____ up a balloon. ● "Rub this on your head," he said. ● The balloon made my _____ stand up _____! ● Then Hoony made the balloon _____ on the wall! ● "What's the _____?" I asked. ● "The balloon has _____ electricity," Hoony said. ● "It's okay to _____ it. ● Static electricity isn't _____," Hoony _____. ● "You can use static electricity to make a lemon _____." ● "We just need a lemon and a few _____," Hoony said.

It was very _____. ● Hoony's brain was very _____ today. ● He was like a real _____.

It's interesting that a lemon can be used as a _____ to create electricity.

■ 녹음을 듣고, 해당하는 단어와 뜻을 쓰세요.

1	단어:	뜻:	2	단어:	뜻:
3	단어:	뜻:	4	단어:	뜻:
5	단어:	뜻:	6	단어:	뜻:
7	단어:	뜻:	8	단어:	뜻:
9	단어:	뜻:	10	단어:	뜻:
11	단어:	뜻:	12	단어:	뜻:
13	단어:	뜻:	14	단어:	뜻:
15	단어:	뜻:	16	단어:	뜻:
17	단어:	뜻:	18	단어:	뜻:
19	단어:	뜻:	20	단어:	뜻:
21	단어:	뜻:	22	단어:	뜻:
23	단어:	뜻:	24	단어:	뜻:
25	단어:	뜻:	26	단어:	뜻:
27	단어:	뜻:	28	단어:	뜻:
29	단어:	뜻:	30	단어:	뜻:

Voca Plus

The universe

1. **comet** 혜성
2. **sun** 태양
3. **Mercury** 수성
4. **Venus** 금성
5. **Earth** 지구
6. **Mars** 화성
7. **Jupiter** 목성
8. **Saturn** 토성
9. **Uranus** 천왕성
10. **Neptune** 해왕성

Culture Plus

Weather 날씨

+ **heavy rain** 폭우   + **lightning** 번개

+ **smog** 스모그

+ **strong wind** 강풍

+ **windstorm** 회오리 바람

+ **tornado** 토네이도

+ **thunder** 천둥

VOCA ED

VOCA EDGE SMART_2

Episode

다이어리에게.

환하고 햇살이 좋은 날이었어. 정말 멋진 만우절이었어! 영어 수업시간에 우리는 "보세요, 쥐예요!"라고 외쳤어. 영어 선생님은 문 밖으로 뛰어나갔어. 하지만 우리는 거짓말했어. 그것은 쥐가 아니라 햄스터였어. 반 아이 중 한 명이 학교로 그것을 가져왔어.

쉬는 시간에 우리는 바닥에 기름을 부었어. 우리는 바닥을 열심히 문질렀어. 우리는 바닥을 미끄럽게 하려고 했어. 드디어 역사 선생님이 교실로 들어오셨어. 나는 걱정이 되었어. 나는 거의 웃지 않았어. 만약 선생님이 균형을 잃고 넘어지시면 어떻게 하지? 구급차를 불러야 할까? 그분은 넘어지지도 화를 내지도 않으셨어. 선생님은 미소를 지으셨고 우리의 장난을 중단시켰어. 그분은 앞을 생각하고 우리의 장난을 예상할 수 있었을까?

Exercise

A

1. 밝은, 화려한
2. 달리다, 뛰다
3. 거짓말하다, 거짓말
4. 가져오다
5. 쉬는 시간
6. 근심하는
7. 거의 ~하지 않다
8. 균형, 균형을 잡다
9. 앞으로, 앞에
10. 장난, 속임수, 재주

B

1. April Fool
2. shout
3. hamster
4. pour
5. rub
6. slippery
7. enter
8. ambulance
9. slip
10. mouse

C

1. April Fool's
2. ran
3. brought
4. poured
5. slippery
6. balance
7. slipped
8. ahead

Episode

보미: 저는 엄마가 친구들과 휴가를 떠나서 기뻐요.
아빠: 그래, 엄마는 이틀 동안 다시 혼자가 되는 거네!
보미: 아빠, 이 복사본을 읽어 보세요. 아빠의 새해 각오들이에요. 엄마는 아빠가 거기에 서명하기를 바라요.
아빠: "나는 잠자리에 들기 전에 운동을 할 것이다." "나는 담배를 끊을 것이다." 으, 네 엄마는 내 매니저 같구나!
보미: 운동을 하면 가끔 더블 치즈버거를 먹을 수 있어요. 담배를 끊으면 달콤한 파이도 먹을 수 있어요. 아빠의 다음 검진 때까지 몸이 훨씬 좋아질 거예요!
아빠: 너의 새해 각오는 가사를 돕는 거지, 그렇지?
보미: 네, 세리, 후니와 제가 일을 나눌 거예요. 저는 쓰레기를 내놓을 거예요. 세리는 식물에 물을 줄 거예요. 그리고 후니는 차고를 청소할 거예요. 지금 저는 후니에게 젓가락 사용법을 알려주고도 있어요.
아빠: 엄마가 무척 좋아하겠구나.

Exercise

A

1. 혼자의, 독신의
2. 사본, 복사한 것
3. 운동하다, 운동
4. ~와 같이, ~처럼
5. 매니저, 관리자
6. 두 배의, 2중의
7. 그만두다, 끊다
8. 가사, 자질구레한 일
9. 나누다
10. 좋아하는, 기쁜

B

1. holiday
2. resolution
3. sign
4. smoke
5. slice
6. checkup
7. garbage
8. plant
9. garage
10. chopsticks

C

1. holiday
2. sign
3. like
4. double
5. Quit
6. chores
7. garage
8. chopsticks

Chapter 1 Unit 3

 Chapter 1 Unit 4

Episode

보미: 수진, 이거 내가 좋아하는 음악 밴드 볼케이노 사진이
니? 우와, 정말 맵시 있다. 그리고 영웅은 정말 멋져.
수진: 나는 그들과 함께 사진을 찍었어. 우리 고모가 방송국
에서 일하시거든. 기자야.
보미: 가끔 그들을 인터뷰도 해?
수진: 물론이지.
보미: 정말 부럽다. 나 대신 선물을 전해 줄 수 있을까?
수진: 글쎄…
보미: 내가 영웅을 위해 티셔츠를 포장했어. 그리고 이것은
그의 생일 축하 카드야.
수진: 그에게 직접 주지 그래?
보미: 너도 알다시피 나는 용감하지 못해. 나는 영웅에게 그
것을 줄 용기가 없어. 솔직히 나는 전에 그들을 만났을
때 한 마디도 못했어. 단지 먼 거리에서 바라만 보았어.
또다시 바보처럼 보이고 싶지 않아.

수진은 내 앞에서 약간 자랑했다. 사실 그 애는 내가 얼마나
볼케이노를 좋아하는지 정확하게 안다. 나는 그 애가 나를
도울 수 있기를 바란다.

Exercise

A

1. 맵시 있는, 멋진
2. 멋진, 굉장한
3. 기자
4. 부러워하다, 질투, 선망
5. 전하다, 배달하다
6. 포장하다
7. 사람, 개인
8. 먼 거리, 먼 곳, 거리
9. 자랑하다
10. 돕다, 거들다, 도움

B

1. favorite
2. photo
3. broadcasting
4. interview
5. congratulation
6. brave
7. courage
8. honestly
9. foolish
10. exactly

C

1. photo
2. broadcasting
3. interview
4. deliver
5. person
6. courage
7. distance
8. boasted

Episode

사라에게,
우리가 처음 만났을 때 기억하니? 우리는 같은 초등학교로
전학을 왔어. 심지어 같은 날짜에 학교에 왔어. 자연스럽게
우리는 친구가 되었어. 만일 우리가 같은 학급이 아니었으면
누가 내 친구가 되었을까? 너는 내 옆에 앉았어. 우리는 생
김새가 닮지 않았는데 우리 반 애들은 우리가 그렇다고 말
했어. 우리는 어떤 면에서는 달라. 너는 요리에 감각이 있지
만, 나는 없어. 나는 너의 토스트를 좋아하고 너는 그것을 태
우지 않고 만들 수 있어. 너는 또한 잼을 고르게 바르는 것을
잘해. 너는 약간 부끄러움을 타지만, 나는 외향적이야. 너는
내게 아주 친절해. 우리는 어떤 점에서는 비슷해. 우리는 같
은 프로그램들을 좋아해. 우리는 여가 시간에 연기하는 것을
즐겨. 가끔 우리는 우주선을 탄 척을 하지. 사라, 미래에 나와
함께 남극에 가자고 한 약속을 절대 잊지 마.

Exercise

A

1. 초등학교의, 입문의
2. 자연스럽게, 당연히
3. 가정하다, 만약 ~이면, 어떨까
4. 바르다, 펴다
5. 고르게, 평평하게
6. 외향적인
7. ~동안
8. 가끔
9. 비슷한, 서로 같은
10. 미래, 앞날

B

1. remember
2. classmate
3. different
4. sense
5. burn
6. friendly
7. similar
8. spare
9. spaceship
10. forget

C

1. date
2. Suppose
3. alike
4. sense
5. spreading
6. outgoing
7. similar
8. Sometimes

1. lie	거짓말하다	
2. pour	붓다	
3. rub	문지르다	
4. anxious	근심하는	
5. bright	밝은, 환한	
6. hardly	거의 ~하지 않다	
7. balance	균형을 잡다, 균형	
8. resolution	결심, 결의	
9. quit	그만두다, 끊다	
10. checkup	건강 진단	
11. chores	가사, 자질구레한 일	
12. divide	나누다	
13. garage	차고	
14. garbage	쓰레기	
15. pleased	좋아하는, 기쁜	
16. favorite	좋아하는	
17. awesome	멋진, 굉장한	
18. envy	부러워하다, 질투	
19. wrap	포장하다	
20. deliver	전하다, 배달하다	
21. courage	용기	
22. honestly	솔직히	
23. foolish	어리석은	
24. boast	자랑하다	
25. exactly	정확하게	
26. elementary	초등학교의, 입문의	
27. alike	비슷한, 서로 같은	
28. evenly	고르게, 평평하게	
29. similar	유사한	
30. sometimes	가끔	

Episode

세리: 야야, 손가락을 베었어! 이봐, 피가 나!
보미: 내가 구급상자를 가져올게. 자 여기, 거기에 이 반창고를 붙여.
세리: 그것은 너무 평범하고 단순해. 나는 그 위에 무언가를 그릴래.
보미: 핫도그를 좀 그리는 게 어때?
세리: 그건 정말 싫어. 아니, 나는 아주 멋진 무늬를 그릴 거야. 이거 아름답지 않아? 그리고 나는구슬을 좀 추가하고 싶어.
보미: 네가 그걸 붙일 수 있게 도와줄게.
세리: 고마워. 내게 디카를 가져다 줘.
보미: 유튜브에 사진을 올릴 거니?
세리: 아니, 나는 그것을 반창고 회사에 보내고 싶어. 그들에게 깊은 인상을 줄지도 모르잖아.
보미: 그것이 그들의 사업에 도움이 될 수 있을 거라고 생각해.

Exercise

A

1. 베다, 상처를 내다, 베기	2. 평범한, 단조로운
3. 단순한, 간단한	4. 불쾌한, 구역질이 나는
5. 추가하다, 더하다	6. 접착제(로 붙이다)
7. 게시하다, 정보를 알리다	8. 깊은 인상을 주다
9. 추측하다, 알아맞히다	10. 응급 치료의

B

1. blood	2. bandage
3. draw	4. hot dog
5. pattern	6. beautiful
7. digital camera	8. send
9. company	10. business

C

1. first-aid	2. bandage
3. plain / simple	4. pattern
5. glue	6. digital camera
7. post	8. guess

Chapter **2** Unit 6

Episode

다이어리에게,
후니가 비눗방울을 부는 모습이 보여. 내가 그것들을 세어 볼게. 그는 둥근 비눗방울을 열 개 불었어. 납작한 비눗방울도 몇 개 불었어. 그는 다른 모양도 만들 수 있어. 그는 자신의 비눗방울 쇼를 위해 연습하고 있어. 사라와 나는 그를 위해 손가락 그림자를 만들어 줄 거야. 우리는 그의 성우도 되어 줄 거야. 우리는 막 뒤에 있을 거야.

보미: 쇼는 예정대로 진행될 거지, 그렇지? 우리가 하이에나를 만들어내는 것을 봐.
후니: 그것들이 하이에나의 날카로운 이빨이야?
보미: 응, 썩은 고기를 먹고 있어. 고기 뼈는 표현하기 힘들었어.
후니: 그래, 정말 머리를 썼네!
보미: 이제 우리가 나뭇가지를 표현하는 것을 봐.
후니: 멋지다! 아, 문 앞에 있는 저 많은 학생들을 봐.
보미: 걱정하지 마. 그들은 네가 전문가라고 생각할 거야!

Exercise

A

1. 세다, 계산하다
2. 모양
3. 연습하다, 연습
4. 막, 휘장
5. 예정, 계획
6. 만들어내다, 창작하다
7. 날카로운
8. 가지
9. 썩은
10. 전문가, 프로의

B

1. blow
2. bubble
3. round
4. flat
5. shadow
6. voice actor
7. bone
8. brain
9. student
10. gate

C

1. blowing
2. practicing
3. shadows
4. voice actors
5. schedule
6. bone
7. brains
8. professional

Chapter **2** Unit 7

Episode

다이어리에게,
할아버지와 나는 과거의 생활에 대해 얘기를 나눴어. 나는 할아버지께 지난 세기에 있었던 몇 가지 변화에 대해 여쭤봤어. 그는 내게 몇 가지에 대해 설명해 주었어.

할아버지: 우리는 이를 뽑기 위해 치과 의사에게 가지 않았어. 집에서 이를 뽑았다는 게 상상이 되니?
보 미: 아, 고통스럽겠어요! 사람들 건강에 해롭지는 않았나요?
할아버지: 전혀 그렇지는 않았어. 그리고 우리는 정기적으로 검진을 받지도 않았어. 20세기에는 역사적인 사건이 많았어. 라이트 형제가 그들의 첫 비행을 했지.
보 미: 그럼 그들이 세계 최초의 조종사였군요.
할아버지: 맞아. 자동차가 대량생산되기 시작했어. 노동자들이 그것을 공장에서 만들었어. 전에는 농부가 많았어. 하지만 곧 공장 기술자가 더 많아졌지.
보 미: 그리고 전화기가 의사 소통에 있어서 큰 변화였어요, 그렇죠?
할아버지: 음, 알렉산더 그레이엄 벨은 한 세기 앞서 그것을 발명했어. 20세기에는 휴대 전화가 대화를 바꿔놓았어.

Exercise

A

1. 일어나다, 발생하다
2. 세기, 100년
3. 상상하다
4. 대량 생산하다
5. 해로운
6. 설명하다
7. 발명하다
8. 일찍이, 예전에
9. 농부
10. 기술자

B

1. past
2. dentist
3. pain
4. historical
5. flight
6. pilot
7. factory
8. communication
9. conversation
10. regular

C

1. occurred
2. explained
3. imagine
4. historical
5. mass-produced
6. communication
7. earlier
8. conversations

1. first-aid	응급 치료의
2. bandage	반창고
3. plain	평범한, 단조로운
4. draw	그리다
5. gross	불쾌한, 구역질이 나는
6. pattern	무늬
7. glue	접착제로 붙이다, 접착제
8. impress	깊은 인상을 주다
9. guess	추측하다, 알아맞히다
10. post	게시하다, 정보를 알리다
11. count	세다, 계산하다
12. blow	불다
13. practice	연습하다, 연습
14. flat	납작한
15. create	만들어내다, 창작하다
16. sharp	날카로운
17. schedule	예정, 계획
18. rotten	썩은
19. professional	전문가, 프로의
20. branch	가지
21. occur	일어나다, 발생하다
22. explain	설명하다
23. century	세기, 100년
24. imagine	상상하다
25. mass-produce	대량 생산하다
26. harmful	해로운
27. historical	역사적인
28. farmer	농부
29. invent	발명하다
30. earlier	일찍이, 예전에

Episode

아빠: 내일 우리는 해안 마을로 떠날 거야. 그곳은 서울에서 멀리 떨어져 있어.

보미: 아빠, 뜨거운 물로 샤워할 수 있나요? 거기에서 맛있는 해산물을 먹을 수 있나요?

아빠: 보미, 우리는 자원 봉사하러 가는 거야.

보미: 뭐라구요? 크리스마스 전날 밤에 자원 봉사를 한다고 요? 아빠, 지금 예수님처럼 "네 이웃을 사랑하라"고 말 씀하시는 거예요?

아빠: 보미, 기름 유출이 있었잖니.

아빠는 갑자기 저녁 식사 때 그것을 알리셨다. 우리는 이른 아 침에 마을에 도착했다. 많은 사람들이 돌들을 씻어내고 있었다. 우리 가족은 한 팀처럼 일을 했다. 나는 해안에서 몇 마리의 새들을 발견했다. 세리와 나는 한 조로 일을 했다. 우리는 그들 의 깃털로부터 기름을 닦아냈다. 우리는 열심히 일했고 식사 조차 걸렀다. 하루가 끝날 무렵에 마을 사람들은 우리에게 감 사를 표시했다. 아빠는 "보미와 세리, 너희들 오늘 정말 열심히 일했구나. 나는 너희가 자랑스럽다"라고 말씀하셨다.

Exercise

A

1. 샤워하다, 잔뜩 주다, 샤워   2. 자원 봉사하다, 지원자
3. 용서하다, 용서   4. 알리다, 발표하다
5. 씻어내다, 헹구다   6. ~에 도착하다
7. 한 쌍, 2인조   8. 열심히 일하는
9. 먼   10. 기름 유출

B

1. village   2. eve
3. neighbor   4. dinner
5. coast   6. feather
7. appreciation   8. meal
9. seafood   10. team

C

1. village   2. Eve
3. neighbors   4. announced
5. rinsing   6. coast
7. meal   8. appreciation

Chapter 3 Unit 9

Chapter 3 Unit 10

Episode

세리: 내 헤어 스프레이를 써보자.

보미: 이봐, 너는 내 머리를 너무 단단하게 만들고 있어.

세리: 보미 언니, 왜 언니는 항상 검정 또는 회색 코트만 입어? 왜 추운 날에 치마를 입어?

보미: 우리는 학교에 헐렁한 바지를 입고 갈 수 없어.

세리: 그것은 불공평해. 언젠가 나는 여자아이들을 위한 교복을 디자인할 거야.

보미: 세리, 이 인쇄물을 봐. 우리 학교의 규칙들이야.

세리: 몇몇 부분에 밑줄을 쳤네. 이 규칙은 왜 있는 거야? 다채로운 코트들은 허용이 안 된다고? 이제 이유를 이해하겠네. 그래서 언니는 그렇게 지루한 코트들을 입는구나. 심지어 사라 언니의 애완 동물도 털을 보라색으로 염색하는 걸 좋아해.

보미: 맞아. 나도 나의 개성을 표현하고 싶어. 왜 중학생들은 그렇게 하는 것이 허용이 안 되지?

Episode

사라: 보미, 나는 '상상해 봐'라는 이 노래가 좋아. 메시지가 있어. 노래에 가사를 더 추가하는게 어때?

보미: 동의해. 전쟁이 없다고 상상해 봐. 우리는 군인들이 필요 없을 거야.

사라: 하지만 누가 우리나라를 지키지?

보미: 그냥 무기가 하나도 없다고 상상해 봐.

사라: 그러면 우리는 평화로울 거야. 나라 사이의 국경도 없을 거야.

보미: 언어가 없다고 상상해 봐.

사라: 우리는 몸짓을 더 사용하게 될 거야. 지도가 없다고 상상해 봐.

보미: 그러면 우리는 세상에 대한 충분한 지식이 없을 거야.

사라: 사막이 어디에 있는지 알 수 없을 거야.

보미: 교육이 없다고 상상해 봐. 우리는 모든 것을 이해하는데 어려움이 있을 거야.

Exercise

A

1. 스프레이, 뿌리다
2. 단단한, 굳은, 회사
3. ~거나 ~거나, 둘 중 하나의
4. 제복, 교복
5. 밑줄을 긋다, 밑줄
6. 규칙, 지배하다
7. 다채로운, 화려한
8. 이유, 설명하다
9. 자주빛의, 보라빛의
10. 허가하다, 허락하다

B

1. skirt
2. loose
3. unfair
4. handout
5. regulation
6. boring
7. dye
8. express
9. personality
10. middle

C

1. firm
2. loose
3. uniforms
4. regulations
5. rule
6. dyed
7. express / personality
8. allowed

Exercise

A

1. 상상하다
2. 동의하다
3. 군인
4. 보호하다, 지키다
5. ~사이에
6. 몸짓
7. 충분한
8. 사막, 불모의, 버리다
9. 어려움
10. 무기

B

1. message
2. line
3. peace
4. border
5. language
6. map
7. knowledge
8. education
9. war
10. enough

C

1. lines
2. war
3. borders
4. gestures
5. enough
6. deserts
7. difficulty
8. protect

1. far	먼
2. volunteer	자원 봉사하다, 지원자
3. pardon	용서하다, 용서
4. neighbor	이웃(사람)
5. rinse	씻어내다, 헹구다
6. reach	~에 도착하다
7. announce	알리다, 발표하다
8. coast	해안
9. meal	식사
10. hardworking	열심히 일하는
11. firm	단단한, 회사
12. loose	헐렁한
13. either	둘 중 하나의
14. regulation	규정
15. colorful	다채로운, 화려한
16. reason	설명하다, 이유
17. boring	지루한
18. dye	염색하다
19. allow	허가하다, 허락하다
20. personality	개성
21. imagine	상상하다
22. agree	동의하다
23. protect	보호하다, 지키다
24. border	국경
25. between	~사이에
26. language	언어
27. enough	충분한
28. knowledge	지식
29. desert	사막, 불모의, 버리다
30. difficulty	어려움

Episode

아빠: 돈을 절약할 수 있는 방법에 대해 의논하자.
보미: 제게 좋은 예가 떠올랐어요. 세리, 무선 전화기로 오래 통화하지 마.
세리: 해 보미 언니는 휴대 전화로 오래 수다 떨지 매
아빠: 그리고 국제 전화는 언제 하는 것이 좋지?
보미: 밤 늦게요. 그때 요금이 더 싸요.
엄마: 그리고 나는 오후 늦게 장보러 가려고 해. 물건이 그때 더 싸거든.
세리: 그리고 재래시장으로 가야죠, 그렇죠?
엄마: 그래. 그곳 물건이 백화점에서보다 더 싸단다. 하지만 백화점 세일을 활용해야지.
보미: 저는 항상 가게 쿠폰을 이용하려고 해요.
후니: 저는 전기를 아끼는 방법을 알아요. 불을 꺼요. 그리고 사용하지 않을 때는 플러그를 빼요.
엄마: 와, 너희 모두 돈을 절약하는 방법에 대해 잘 알고 있구나!

Exercise

A

1. 보기, 예
2. 무선의
3. 국제적인, 국제간의
4. 수다를 떨다, 담소
5. 물건 사기, 장보기
6. 물품, 상품
7. 플러그를 뽑다
8. 현명한, 박식한
9. 세일, 할인행사
10. 절약하다, 아끼다

B

1. night
2. cheaper
3. outdoor
4. market
5. department store
6. electricity
7. turn
8. light
9. money
10. coupon

C

1. save
2. wireless
3. international
4. outdoor
5. department stores
6. sales
7. electricity
8. unplug

Chapter 4 Unit 12

Chapter 4 Unit 13

Episode

보미: 나는 볼케이노 콘서트 티켓을 살 수 없어. 나는 티켓에 5만원 이상 쓸 수 없어.

사라: 나도 표를 살 돈이 안돼. 티켓이 너무 비싸!

보미: 저기, 저 광고 좀 봐. 저 개가 스케이트보드를 타고 있어.

사라: 새로운 모델을 뽑고 있다고 하네. 우승자들에게 상금을 준대. 우리 브라우니를 참가시키자!

보미: 그래, 브라우니가 이 스케이트보드 위에 포즈를 취하게 하자.

사라: 브라우니에게 이 선글라스를 씌워 봐. 좋아, 내가 사진을 찍을게.

보미: 어! 브라우니는 스케이트보드 위에 서 있는 것을 몹시 싫어해. 진정해, 브라우니. 너를 화나게 하고 싶지 않아. 이렇게 빌게, 브라우니!

사라: 그래, 드디어 찍었어! 잘했어, 브라우니!

보미: 잘됐다, 우리가 해낸 거야! 수고했어, 브라우니!

사라: 자 여기, 상으로 참치 좀 먹어.

보미: 우유 먹어, 브라우니. 목말라 보여.

Exercise

A

1. 표, 입장권
2. 소비하다, 지출
3. ~할 여유가 있다
4. (경기 등에) 참가시키다
5. 자세를 취하다, 자세(포즈)
6. 사진을 찍다, 사진
7. 화나게 하다, 노여움, 화
8. 빌다, 간청하다
9. 임무 완수, 역할
10. 목마른, 갈망하는

B

1. expensive
2. skateboard
3. prize
4. hate
5. stand
6. excellent
7. succeed
8. reward
9. concert
10. ad(advertisement)

C

1. spend
2. afford
3. models
4. pose
5. photograph
6. hates
7. anger
8. reward

Episode

세리에게.

너 오늘 정말 귀엽다, 세리. 너는 정말로 마음이 따뜻한 사람이야. 제발 숨을 크게 쉬고 내 말을 좀 들어줘. 너의 새 MP3 플레이어 있잖아? 음, 내가 그걸 빌려서 학교에 가져갔었어. 모든 애들의 시선을 사로잡았어. 같은 반 애들은 그게 아주 멋지다고 생각했어. 그런데 체육 시간이 끝나고 돌아오니 그것이 내 가방 안에 없었어. 누군가가 훔쳐갔어! 우리는 도둑을 못 찾았어. 아, 나는 엄마의 조언을 들었어야 했어. 엄마는 그걸 집에 두고 가는 게 좋겠다고 하셨거든. 이봐, 내가 좋아하는 재킷이 이제 네 거야. 너에게 딱 맞을 거야. 어차피 나에게는 조금 끼었거든. 그건 아주 유명한 브랜드야. 2년 정도 되었다는 것을 제외하면 완벽해. 그러니 그것을 갖고 제발 나를 용서해 줘!

Exercise

A

1. 인정이 있는, 친절한
2. 아주 새로운, 신품의
3. 주의, 주목
4. 멋진, 시원한
5. 되돌아오다(가다)
6. 조언, 충고
7. 남기다, 두고 가다(오다)
8. ~에 꼭 맞다, 어울리다
9. 어쨌든, 아무튼
10. ~를 제외하고

B

1. deep
2. breath
3. borrow
4. steal
5. thief
6. favorite
7. bit
8. tight
9. famous
10. forgive

C

1. cute
2. deep
3. attention
4. returned
5. advice
6. bit / anyway
7. except
8. forgive

1. save	절약하다, 아끼다
2. wireless	무선의
3. chat	수다를 떨다, 담소
4. international	국제적인, 국제간의
5. goods	상품, 물품
6. cheaper	값이 더 싼
7. outdoor	야외의
8. example	보기, 예
9. unplug	플러그를 뽑다
10. wise	현명한, 박식한
11. spend	쓰다, 지출, 비용
12. afford	~할 여유가 있다
13. expensive	비싼
14. prize	상, 포상
15. photograph	사진을 찍다, 사진
16. hate	몹시 싫어하다
17. enter	(경기 등에) 참가시키다
18. excellent	훌륭한
19. beg	빌다, 간청하다
20. thirsty	목마른, 갈망하는
21. warm-hearted	인정이 있는, 친절한
22. breath	숨, 호흡
23. borrow	빌리다
24. attention	주의, 주목
25. thief	도둑
26. bit	조각, 조금
27. leave	남기다, 두고 가다
28. famous	유명한
29. except	~를 제외하고, ~외에는
30. forgive	용서하다

Episode

다이어리에게,
사라와 나는 시내에 갔어. 지금 우리는 로봇 콘테스트에 와 있어. 와, 로봇은 많은 것들을 할 수 있어. 몇몇 로봇들은 심지어 가구도 운반할 수 있어.

사라: 저 로봇 봐. 사람들에게 인사하고 있어! 다리도 구부릴 수 있어.
보미: 나는 그 로봇의 친절한 미소가 좋아.
시라: 로봇이 종이의 장 수를 세고 있어.
보미: 이봐, 저기 있는 로봇은 음식을 내고 있어. 그리고 그 옆에 있는 로봇은 무엇인가를 섞고 있어. 밀가루와 계란을 섞고 있어.
사라: 기계보다는 사람처럼 생겼어. 그 발명가들은 천재들임에 틀림이 없어.
보미: 나는 아담한 로봇을 원해. 무겁지 않았으면 좋겠어. 그것이 청소를 도와준다면 나는 친구들을 더 자주 초대할 거야.
사라: 그 로봇은 똑똑해야겠네. 나는 그 로봇이 우리를 학교까지 운전해서 데려다 줄 수 있으면 좋겠어.

Exercise

A
1. 도심지로, 시내, 도심지
2. 대회, 경연, 콘테스트
3. 많음, 많은
4. 나르다, 운반하다
5. 음식을 내다, 음식 시중을 들다
6. 혼합하다, 섞다
7. 자주, 종종
8. 영리한, 똑똑한
9. 운전하다, 드라이브
10. 인사하다

B
1. thing
2. furniture
3. bend
4. sheet
5. flour
6. machine
7. genius
8. compact
9. heavy
10. invite

C
1. plenty
2. carry
3. greeting
4. serving
5. machine
6. geniuses
7. invite
8. clever

Chapter 5 Unit 15

REVIEW TEST Unit 14~ Unit 15

Episode

다이어리에게,
우리 할머니는 정말로 현대 기술을 즐기셔. 작년에 엄마가 나의
졸업식에 참석하지 못하셨어. 그래서 할머니는 나를 기분 좋게
하려고 노력하셨어. 졸업식을 하는 동안 할머니께서는 '치즈'라
고 말씀하시면서 나의 사진을 찍으셨어.

할머니: 보미, 내 휴대 전화로 사진 찍는 것이 정말 편리하구나.
보 미: 할머니가 현대 문명을 즐기시니 정말 멋져요.
할머니: 나는 컴퓨터를 대여하고 싶어. 나는 동호회 회원들에게
　　　　메시지를 보낼 수가 없어.
보 미: 할머니, 컴퓨터에 무슨 문제가 있나요?
할머니: 그것이 고장이 나서 정비사를 불렀어.
보 미: 도서관에서 컴퓨터 사용하실 수 있으세요. 그런데, 할머니.
　　　　점점 더 사교적으로 변하시네요. 인터넷 낚시 동호회 소
　　　　속이세요?
할머니: 그럼. 지난달에 가입했어. 너도 알다시피 할아버지와
　　　　나는 낚시를 좋아해.
보 미: 그럼 할머니는 낚시 동호회 회원이네요. 낚시에 관한 정
　　　　보도 많이 얻나요?
할머니: 물론이지. 할아버지와 나는 회원들하고 다음 달에 섬으
　　　　로 낚시를 갈 거야.
보 미: 두 분은 정말 에너지가 넘치세요.

Exercise

A
1. 현대의
2. 격려하다, 환호, 격려
3. 식, 의식
4. 대여하다, 집세, 임대료
5. 문제, 중요하다
6. 수선, 수리하다
7. ~에 속하다, 소속하다
8. 지난, 마지막의
9. 가득 찬
10. 졸업

B
1. technology
2. convenient
3. culture
4. member
5. library
6. sociable
7. join
8. information
9. island
10. picture

C
1. modern
2. graduation
3. convenient
4. repair
5. sociable
6. belong
7. fishing
8. information

1. plenty	많음, 많은
2. thing	물건, 것
3. carry	나르다, 운반하다
4. furniture	가구
5. greet	인사하다
6. bend	구부리다
7. mix	혼합하다, 섞다
8. flour	밀가루
9. serve	음식 시중을 들다
10. sheet	한 장, 시트
11. genius	천재
12. compact	아담한
13. often	자주, 종종
14. invite	초대하다
15. clever	영리한, 똑똑한
16. modern	현대의
17. cheer	격려하다, 환호, 격려
18. graduation	졸업
19. ceremony	식, 의식
20. convenient	편리한
21. matter	중요성, 문제가 되다
22. library	도서관
23. repair	수리하다, 수선
24. sociable	사교성 있는
25. rent	대여하다, 임대료
26. belong	~에 속하다
27. join	가입하다
28. information	정보
29. island	섬
30. last	지난, 마지막의

Episode

보미: 우리는 수업시간에 재미있는 주제를 토론했어. 오염에 대해 이야기했어.

사라: 그건 요새 중요한 세계적 문제야.

보미: 환경은 아주 중요한 거잖아. 늘 우리에게 영향을 미치는 거니까. 그리고 환경은 우리 모두를 똑같이 취급해. 우리 모두 똑같게 영향을 받아. 모든 사람이 할 수 있는 건 우리가 배출하는 쓰레기의 양을 줄이는 거야.

사라: 그래. 우리는 물건을 재사용할 수 있어. 내 새로운 지갑을 좀 봐. 나는 옛날 청바지를 사용해서 그걸 만들었어.

보미: 청바지가 유행이 지난 거였니?

사라: 응, 하지만 이제는 지갑으로 여전히 유용해!

보미: 우리 엄마는 우리 집 비누를 만드셔. 엄마는 사용한 식용유로 비누를 만드시는 거야.

사라: 우리 엄마는 빈 플라스틱 병을 다시 쓰셔. 그 안에 식물을 키우셔. 나는 가끔 엄마를 도와 꽃씨를 심기도 해. 곧 병에서 꽃들이 나기 시작할 거야.

Exercise

A

1. 토론하다, 논의하다
2. 세계적인, 전 세계의
3. ~에 영향을 미치다, 영향
4. 똑같게, 균등하게
5. 다시 사용하다, 재사용
6. 기르다, 재배하다
7. 씨앗, 씨를 뿌리다
8. 싹트다, 나기 시작하다, 싹
9. 공해, 오염
10. 대우하다, 취급하다

B

1. topic
2. environment
3. reduce
4. wallet
5. jeans
6. useful
7. soap
8. cooking oil
9. empty
10. bottle

C

1. discussed
2. environment
3. treats
4. reduce
5. wallet
6. fashion
7. cooking oil
8. sprout

Episode

다이어리에게.

아빠와 나는 신문에서 재미있는 기사를 살펴보고 있어. 그것은 여가 활동에 관한 거야. 내일 열기구 축제가 있을 거야. 우리는 열기구를 탈까 생각 중이야. 사방의 아름다운 풍경을 감상할 수 있어. 몸과 마음에 도움이 될 거야.

기사에 의하면 열기구 비행사가 있대. 그는 열기구를 조정해. 열기구는 가스로 채워져. 가끔 비행사가 열기구를 부풀리는 일을 도와주게 해준대! 열기구가 비행을 시작한 후 열기구 비행사가 그것을 통제하고 정해진 경로를 따라가. 한 시간쯤 후에 그는 안전하게 땅 위로 열기구를 착륙시킬 거야. 보통 열기구는 사고로부터 안전해. 게다가 내일 일기예보가 아주 좋아. 내일 바람이 약할 거래. 이것은 무슨 의미일까? 열기구 타기에 딱 좋은 날씨라는 거야!

Exercise

A

1. 기사, 논설
2. 여가, 자유시간
3. 열기구, 타기
4. (풍선 등을) 부풀게 하다
5. 경로, 진로
6. 착륙시키다, 육지
7. 예보, 예상, 예보하다
8. 온화한, 순한
9. 완벽한, 완성하다
10. 활동, 운동

B

1. paper
2. hot-air balloon
3. scenery
4. mind
5. balloonist
6. pilot
7. control
8. accident
9. mean
10. fill

C

1. article
2. leisure
3. scenery
4. pilots
5. inflate
6. land
7. forecast
8. wind

Chapter 6 Unit 18

REVIEW TEST Unit 16~ Unit 18

Episode

다이어리에게,
후니와 나는 막 나가려는 참이었어. 그런데 갑자기 비가 오기 시작했어. 우리는 천둥소리도 들을 수 있었어. 후니는 실험을 하고 싶어했어. "내가 리더를 할래." 그가 말했어. 우선, 후니가 풍선 하나를 불었어. "이것을 머리 위에 문질러봐." 그가 말했어. 풍선이 내 머리카락을 곧게 서도록 만들었어! 그리고 후니는 풍선을 벽에 붙게 했어! "비밀이 뭐야?" 나는 물었어. "풍선에 정전기가 생긴 거야." 그가 말했어. "그것을 만져도 괜찮아. 정전기는 위험하지 않아." 후니가 설명했어. "정전기를 이용해서 레몬 전지를 만들 수 있어." "그냥 레몬과 몇 가지 도구만 있으면 돼."라고 후니가 말했어.
아주 이상했어. 오늘 후니의 두뇌활동이 매우 활발했어. 그는 진짜 과학자 같았어. 레몬이 전기를 일으키는 매체로 사용될 수 있다니 재미있어.

Exercise

A
1. 지금 막 ~하려고 한다
2. 실험하다, 실험
3. 듣다, 들리다
4. 곧은, 똑바로 선
5. 붙이다, 찌르다
6. 만지다, 촉감
7. 정적인, 정전기의
8. 이상한, 묘한
9. 활동적인, 활발한
10. 매체, 매개물

B
1. suddenly
2. thunder
3. blow
4. hair
5. secret
6. dangerous
7. explain
8. battery
9. tool
10. scientist

C
1. were about to
2. experiment
3. leader
4. hair
5. stick
6. dangerous
7. static
8. scientist

1. discuss	토론하다, 논의하다	
2. pollution	공해, 오염	
3. affect	~에 영향을 미치다, 영향	
4. environment	환경	
5. treat	대우하다, 취급하다	
6. reduce	줄이다	
7. reuse	다시 사용하다, 재사용	
8. empty	텅 빈	
9. sprout	싹트다, 나기 시작하다, 싹	
10. bottle	병	
11. article	기사, 논설	
12. leisure	여가, 자유시간	
13. balloon ride	열기구 타기	
14. scenery	풍경	
15. pilot	조정하다	
16. control	통제하다	
17. inflate	(풍선 등을) 부풀게 하다	
18. accident	사고	
19. forecast	예보, 예상, 예보하다	
20. mean	의미하다	
21. suddenly	갑자기	
22. thunder	천둥	
23. experiment	실험, 실험하다	
24. blow	불다	
25. straight	곧은, 똑바로 선	
26. stick	붙이다, 찌르다	
27. static	정적인, 정전기의	
28. explain	설명하다	
29. strange	이상한, 묘한	
30. medium	매체, 매개물	